POCKET
GARDENING
GUIDES

GREENHOUSES

❖

DAVID SQUIRE

POCKET
GARDENING
GUIDES

GREENHOUSES

❖

DAVID SQUIRE

Illustrated by Vana Haggerty

TIGER BOOKS INTERNATIONAL
LONDON

Designed and conceived by

THE BRIDGEWATER BOOK COMPANY LTD

Art Directed by PETER BRIDGEWATER

Designed by TERRY JEAVONS

Illustrated by VANA HAGGERTY FLS

Edited by MARGOT RICHARDSON

CLB 3371

This edition published in 1994 by

TIGER BOOKS INTERNATIONAL PLC, London

© 1994 Colour Library Books Ltd,

Godalming, Surrey

Printed and bound in Singapore

ISBN 1-85501-380-0

CONTENTS

EARLY TIMES

◆

NEARLY two thousand years ago the ingenious Romans experimented to encourage the early flowering of roses. They made greenhouses roofed in selenite, a type of gypsum formed of transparent crystals. Some of these were warmed by hot air; another method was to dig channels 'two hands wide' around them which were filled with hot water twice a day. An alternative 'greenhouse' was formed by digging a pit and covering it with thin sheets of mica or talc. Many centuries later this probably led to

Greenhouses in the middle of the 1800s enabled a wealth of new plants to be grown. Illustration from The Flower Garden and Greenhouse, *1851.*

the term 'pit light', a heavy, wooden-framed structure with small panes of glass. It was widely used in horticulture until the middle of the 1900s; then replaced by a lighter, single-pane, Dutch type of frame. With the fall of the Roman Empire, the desire to grow plants out of their natural seasons diminished. Later, references in 1259 describe roses and lilies being grown under glass in Padua, north-east Italy. By the fourteenth century, 'glass pavilions' were used in France.

WARDIAN CASES

During the late 1820s, keen naturalist and amateur botanist Dr. Nathaniel Bagshaw Ward discovered, while trying to pupate a moth, that some plants could be grown successfully in enclosed environments, such as glass bottles. Water, transpired from plants and condensed on the inside of the glass, re-moistened the compost. There was also an exchange of gases: carbon dioxide given off during

respiration was reabsorbed during the growth process known as photosynthesis; any oxygen was given off during photosynthesis.

The doctor experimented further and constructed glass cabinets: ornate ones were use to decorate homes, while others transported plants to and from other countries. The ornate Wardian Case illustrated here was featured in 1845 in Every Lady Her Own Flower Gardener. *These cabinets became parts of many Victorian rooms, especially where the air was polluted by smoke.*

ORANGERIES

Orange trees were introduced to England from France in 1562, but needed protection from weather during winter. Eventually, special greenhouses were designed. Initially, however, orange trees were covered by 'wooden tabernacles' and heated by stoves. At the Oxford Botanic Garden in about 1630, orange trees in containers were trundled around fires in wooden sheds in winter and positioned outdoors in summer. Later, glass structures – known as orangeries – were specifically designed, eventually leading to glass roofs and sides and the first great conservatories.

In Northern Europe, orangeries were also popular and used to house figs as well as oranges, while in Germany they gained additional popularity as places for concerts and all kinds of theatrical entertainments.

WHAT'S IN A NAME?

The English gardener John Evelyn first coined the term greenhouse (see page 41), but a contemporary, Sir Thomas Hanmer, used the terms winter-house and winter-room, known in France as *la serre*.

At night, the building was warmed in winter by stoves or pans of hot coals and Sir Thomas warned that these must be used with care as more plants might be killed than preserved. Lack of fresh air was also a problem. He recommended that the place should be lofty, with large windows and doors only on the warm, sunny side. These were to be opened on mild days to let in warm air but closed during frosty weather. The glass was covered by mats at night: placing rolls of hessian on pit lights during frosty nights continued well into the twentieth century.

GLASS TAX

The glass industry in England – which held the key to the development and spread of greenhouses and conservatories – remained virtually stagnant between 1792 and 1845, due to draconian taxation. It was imposed under an austerity budget by William Pitt the Younger, and often referred to as the 'window tax'. Although a few botanical showplaces were constructed before the tax's abolition, afterwards there was a sudden and rapid expansion of greenhouses and conservatories. The number of glass manufacturers in England then started to rise again after falling to only one hundred and twenty-six. Of these, only four or five made plate glass.

The 'Domical Botanic Hot-house', built in England in 1829, cost more than £14,000 due to the high cost of glass. This illustration appeared in 1829 in The Gardener's Magazine.

During the late 1810s, John Loudon invented a greenhouse formed of flexible iron glazing bars. Here is an early design featured in The Greenhouse Companion *in 1824.*

ON A GRAND SCALE

Sir Joseph Paxton (1804–65) was a brilliant gardener, author and architect.

IN AN age of expansion and industrial revolution, when engineers and inventors were practically idolized, it is not surprising that greenhouse and conservatory development also benefited. From the middle of the seventeenth century in Europe, and especially in England, there began social and economic changes that brought about the mechanization of production. By the middle of the following century, changes were gaining speed and by the 1850s the pattern of industrial production practically complete.

Joseph Paxton, later knighted, was the father of 'grand-scale' conservatories. In the 1830s he designed and constructed one measuring 83m/272ft long by 37m/121ft wide and 20m/66ft high at Chatsworth, the home of the Duke of Devonshire. A few years later he designed the Exhibition Building in Hyde Park, opened in 1851 and soon christened the 'Crystal Palace' by the magazine *Punch*. More than six million people visited the exhibition. Large-scale developments also took place in Europe.

On the grand scale, few greenhouses have been as extensive as those at Versailles, a few miles west of Paris. In 1685, a huge orangery was constructed, 155m/509ft long, 12.8m/42ft wide and 13.7m/45ft high. It had a south-facing wall, plenty of windows and a solid roof, and housed more than 1200 orange trees and hundreds of other plants.

Winter gardens – where 'evergreens' and plants that flower from early winter to spring could be grown – were natural progressions from Sir Joseph Paxton's Crystal Palace in 1851. Like the earlier orangeries in Germany, they became places for concerts as well as plants, although later when the gardens were used for dancing and roller-skating, the plants were confined to containers. Below is an 1884 engraving from The Gardeners' Chronical.

MOBILE GLASSHOUSES

During the 1950s and 60s, mobile glasshouses gained prominence in commercial horticulture in temperate regions, enabling crops to be raised earlier than normal as well as late-season plants to be covered while maturing.

They were made of strong, extruded aluminium, with a cantilever design that formed a clear span frequently 10.5m/34ft or more wide. They ran on rails, and when initially constructed functioned well, but with age and the settlement of supports often became stationary.

An early design, built on the 'Paxtonian' system and featured in The Amateur's Greenhouse and Conservatory *in 1873. It allowed in a maximum amount of light.*

The idea of a mobile structure was not new. In 1856, *The Cottage Gardener* advertised a moveable greenhouse designed by Mr. Spencer, gardener to the Marquess of Lansdowne. He claimed 'such a structure is desirable for a tenant who has an unreasonable landlord'.

COW POWER

Few early ways to heat greenhouses have been as ingenious as a Russian system, detailed in *A New System of Practical Domestic Economy* in 1825. It was reported that in Russia, and especially in the vicinity of St. Petersburg, greenhouses were no longer being heated by fuel or steam, but by the breath of cattle! Its superiority, it was claimed, was proven when in a climate where twenty-four degrees of frost are known, vegetables raised in greenhouses heated in this manner were far superior to anything previously grown.

The byre containing the cattle was attached to the greenhouse and constructed with small holes just above the cattle's nostrils, so that expelled warm air would pass directly into the greenhouse. The pressure of the expelled air opened flaps between the byre and greenhouses.

It was further claimed that the cattle's breath provided both great warmth and humidity and so completely eliminated the need to water plants.

Experiments like this were happening throughout Europe, in a vibrant age of discovery, invention and innovation.

WINDOW CONSERVATORIES

Victorian gardeners were highly innovative, creating gardens in glass containers and draping balconies with all sorts of plants. But perhaps they were never so innovative as with window conservatories. These produced a closed environment – except for a ventilator – and were positioned on a window sill where they enveloped the entire area in glass. At the backs of houses they were frequently used to block out unattractive views.

RANGE OF GREENHOUSES

❖

THERE are greenhouses to suit gardens of all sizes and shapes. Mini-greenhouses are ideal in small gardens and on patios while on a grander scale, free-standing types enable a wider range of plants to be grown. Sunrooms and conservatories also introduce a new gardening dimension and are especially suitable for growing large, long-term foliage plants, such as palms.

SHAPES AND SIZES

Whatever the size of greenhouse you initially estimate to suit your needs, double it! Invariably, after gardening in a greenhouse for several months, you will wish to extend the range of plants.

The smaller the greenhouse the more rapid and extreme the tem-perature changes. Those at mid-day and during the afternoon may be excessive, while at night they fall suddenly. A greenhouse about 3.6m/12ft long and 2.4m/8ft wide is about the optimum size, having a volume of air that avoids sudden temperature changes.

There also must be provision for adequate ventilation, and this is discussed on pages 22 and 23.

The range of greenhouses now available includes:

• <u>Full-span greenhouses</u>, with a ridge and two eaves, are traditional and widely available. Wooden and earlier types often have bricks or wooden panels up to about 75cm/2¹/₂ft high. Modern, aluminium-framed types, however, are completely glazed. Greenhouses up to 2.4m/8ft wide have central paths about 60cm/2ft wide and 90cm/3ft-wide spaces on either side for staging or growing plants at ground level.

FULL-SPAN *(also known as even-span) greenhouses have traditional outlines, with a ridge and two eaves. Earlier ones had brick sides up to about 75cm/2¹/₂ft high, but recent types, especially when made of aluminium, have glass from ground to eaves. An alternative to bricks is wood. Most free-standing greenhouses are now full-span types, although three-quarter types are sold − one side is wider than the other.*

LEAN-TO *greenhouses utilize warm, sunny walls both to economize on materials and for the warmth they retain and reflect. Many lean-to types have brick or wooden sides up to about 75cm/ 2¹/₂ft high.*

HEXAGONAL *greenhouses are of a more recent design and have the advantage of absorbing the sun's rays from many angles. Some of these greenhouses have a wooden or brick framework at their bases; others are completely glazed.*

A PLACE TO RELAX

Increasingly, conservatories and sunrooms are constructed as extensions to homes, and create places in which to relax and grow plants. A range of long-lived foliage plants and seasonal flowering ones combines continuity of interest with regular changes.

• <u>Lean-to types</u> vary in length and width to suit the wall or house they are constructed against. Most have brick or wooden walls up to 75cm/2½ft high, with a framework in wood or aluminium. Traditional types are 1.8m/6ft to 2.1m/7ft wide, but some – a compromise between mini-greenhouses and normal lean-to types – are 1.2m/4ft wide, and only large enough for a path and a few shelves.

Some lean-to greenhouses are large enough to form sunrooms and conservatories. Modern forms of these have assumed ornate Victorian styles, with double-glazing and a plastic framework. These create comfortable living areas for plants and people, but ensure they provide plenty of ventilation, in both the sides and roof. Too often, conservatory designers appear more concerned with heat conservation than releasing excessively hot air in summer, which soon kills plants and makes living in them unbearable.

INDIVIDUAL *Dutch lights are, commercially, frequently formed into greenhouses, sometimes as temporary constructions but often as permanent features. They allow plenty of light to enter greenhouses and are ideal for plants growing directly in the soil. Lettuces and tomatoes are popular crops to grow in them, as they thrive on a large amount of light.*

PLASTIC *tunnels are made from heavy-gauge, clear or opaque plastic sheeting stretched over giant metal hoops and secured at ground level. Three or four years is usually the maximum life of the sheeting.*

MINIATURE *lean-to greenhouses are increasingly popular, especially in small gardens and on patios. They are only about 60cm/2ft deep and 1.5m/5ft to the eaves. They are stood on bricks, and for safety, firmly secured to a wall.*

FRAMING AND FLOORING

❖

ALTHOUGH some greenhouses have been made of steel (which soon corrodes) and modern conservatories are double-glazed and have decay-proof plastic-type frames, to most gardeners the choice of a greenhouse is between wood and aluminium. Plastic tunnels are used commercially, but in a garden lack permanency and the attractive visual appeal of traditional wooden greenhouses.

TIMBER CONSTRUCTIONS

The life expectancy of timber-framed greenhouses depends on the type of timber used and its maintenance. Baltic redwood, also known as yellow deal, is frequently used but needs regular painting, as well as being initially treated with a wood preservative. If neglected, extremes of temperature, both inside and outside, as well as high humidity, peel paint off the glazing bars. Additionally, the wood may eventually warp and both doors and ventilators cease to fit properly, allowing in draughts.

Western red cedar is more durable, but instead of being preserved by coats of white paint is coated in linseed oil. And rust-proof brass or galvanized nails are used in its construction.

Oak and teak have been used and are long lasting. Unfortunately, they are prohibitively expensive materials. Many early Victorian conservatories were constructed from these woods and lasted well into this century.

WOODEN FRAMEWORK

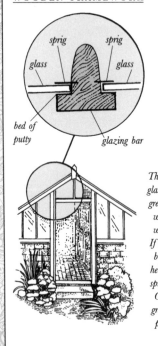

sprig   *sprig*

glass   *glass*

bed of putty   *glazing bar*

ALUMINIUM FRAMEWORK

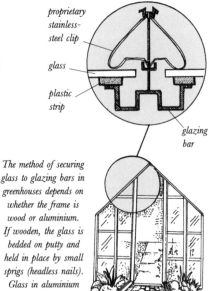

proprietary stainless-steel clip

glass

plastic strip

glazing bar

The method of securing glass to glazing bars in greenhouses depends on whether the frame is wood or aluminium. If wooden, the glass is bedded on putty and held in place by small sprigs (headless nails). Glass in aluminium greenhouses is held by proprietary stainless steel clips.

If the border soil is free from pests or diseases, plants such as tomatoes can be grown directly in it

Solid-based staging is ideal for plants in summer, helping to create a humid atmosphere around them

Slatted staging is ideal for plants in winter, helping to create a flow of air around them

Growing-bags are ideal if the border soil is comtaminated with pests or diseases

Watering-cans with long spouts enable plants at the backs of staging to be reached

Paths may be formed of paving slabs placed either directly on soil or a bed of sand

Store pots, seed-trays and boxes under staging. But ensure they are clean and not contaminated with pests or diseases

ALUMINIUM FRAMEWORK

Most greenhouses are now made of aluminium and have the advantage of not needing any maintenance. Additionally, the supporting framework and glazing bars can be narrower than wooden ones, enabling more light to reach the plants. This is especially beneficial during autumn, winter and also in the early spring.

FLOORING

The easiest way to create a path is to lay paving-slabs either directly on the soil or a layer of sand. If, at sometime later, the layout of the greenhouse needs to be changed, they can be moved.

Conservatories, of course, need more permanent flooring and this is provided by concrete with tiles or some other surface on top.

RAISING THE ROOF

Positioning the roofing trusses of the glass Exhibition Building, later to be known as the Crystal Palace, demanded power and precision. The building, constructed in Hyde Park, London, was opened by Queen Victoria on May Day, 1851.

GLAZING MATERIALS

❖

Although initially expensive during the early 1800s, glass has proved to be the best covering for greenhouses, sunrooms and conservatories. The greatest impetus to its use in Britain was the abolition of the glass tax in the mid-1800s and the construction of the glass-clad Exhibition Hall for the Great Exhibition of 1851.

Early greenhouses had panes of glass 30cm/12in or less wide, but when glass-making techniques improved these became 45cm/1¹/₂ft wide and are now frequently 60cm/2ft across. The use of wider panes was made possible by the introduction of extruded aluminium glazing bars, which are both stronger and lighter than wooden types.

Glass used in greenhouses must be free from bubbles, with a standard weight of 7.32kg/sq cm (24oz/sq ft). The total weight of glass in a greenhouse is considerable, giving the framework rigidity as well as weight to resist winds and storms.

When clean, only 75–80% of the available light passes through, but if dirty this decreases dramatically. In summer, this reduction is not a problem, as the glass will probably be covered in a shading material, but in winter and spring all available light is needed.

THE GREENHOUSE EFFECT

Radiation from the sun contains infra-red radiation as well as visible and ultra-violet radiation. When this radiation reaches a greenhouse, the glass reflects long-wavelength infra-red radiation, but allows short-wavelength infra-red

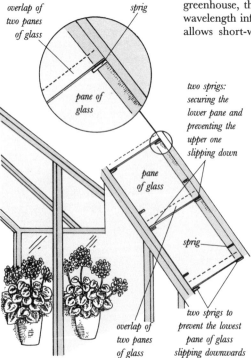

overlap of two panes of glass

sprig

pane of glass

two sprigs: securing the lower pane and preventing the upper one slipping down

pane of glass

sprig

two sprigs to prevent the lowest pane of glass slipping downwards

overlap of two panes of glass

SECURING THE GLASS
Aluminium-framed greenhouses are glazed using proprietary clips (page 12), but wooden greenhouses need a different technique. Individual panes of glass are bedded on a thin, even layer of putty, then held in place with small sprigs. Each pane is secured by four sprigs; the upper two also prevent the pane above slipping downwards. Glaze the roof from the eaves to the ridge, to enable the panes of glass to overlap.

radiation as well as visible light to pass through. These are then absorbed by the soil and plants, thereby raising the temperature. Additionally, infra-red radiation emitted by the soil and plants is of a longer wavelength and does not pass back out through the glass. Therefore it becomes trapped inside the greenhouse, thereby causing the temperature to rise.

SHATTERPROOF GREENHOUSES

Shatterproof materials, such as moulded polycarbonate, have been used in glazing the upper parts of greenhouses, with lower and less vulnerable panels fitted with glass.

Hooped tunnels are covered with sheets of clear or opaque plastic, but they do not have the good warmth-retention properties of glass and after a few years discolour and perish due to the action of ultra-violet light. In commercial horti-culture, these structures are very pop-ular and create inexpensive protection for plants.

If this continued, the temperature within a greenhouse would become unbearable. Therefore, provision must be made to open up ventilators to make the temperature suitable for the plants. Low external temperatures, and wind and rain are also resonsible for decreasing temperatures within the greenhouse and make heating the structure very expensive.

OTHER GLAZING MATERIALS

Many materials other than glass have been used to create a clear covering for greenhouses. Indeed, the Romans some two thousand years ago use thin sheets of mica in frames to cover plants.

Sheets of polycarbonate, 3mm/^{1}/$_8$in thick are amazingly strong – thick sheets are said to be bullet-proof! – and about one-third of the weight of glass. But although tough and initially allow-ing about 85% of light to pass through, it deteriorates after about fifteen years and eventually its structure breaks down.

Acrylic is slightly cheaper but unfortunately also has the ageing problems of polycarbonate.

GLASS BLOWING

In 1845, the British glass-making industry had a swingeing tax removed and glass immediately began a revival in greenhouses and conservatories. Before this, only great estates could afford to construct glasshouses. At the end of the nineteenth century, some greenhouses at the Royal Botanic Gardens, Kew, were glazed with green glass to prevent the sun's rays scorching plants, but when plants under clear glass grew faster, it was removed.

STAGING AND SHELVING

CREATING surfaces on which plants can be displayed is important, as well as forming working areas where seed sowing, potting and other tasks can be performed at a convenient level, about hip or waist height.

In some greenhouses, the staging is a permanent feature, especially for displaying plants such as orchids where it is often tiered. Increasingly, however, flexibility of use is all important: many aluminium greenhouses have hinged shelves that can be lowered to allow plants growing at ground-level to develop.

The range of staging has widened dramatically in recent years and includes:
• <u>Traditional</u> – especially in wooden greenhouses – staging is formed of 5cm/2in-wide wood slats with about 2.5cm/1in between them. This creates a flow of air around plants and is especially beneficial in winter when moisture lingering on leaves readily encourages the presence of diseases. The slatted base also enables the free drainage of surplus water if plants have been excessively watered.
• <u>Small-mesh</u>, galvanized or plastic-covered netting nailed to a wooden framework also creates an airy base, but after several years tends to sag between the supports. Nevertheless, it is relatively inexpensive and quick to construct.
• <u>Solid staging</u>, where a continuous, firm base is covered with a shallow layer of pea-sized gravel chippings is ideal in summer. The chippings retain moisture and create humidity around plants. Alpine plants are frequently buried to their rims in the gravel, which also helps to keep their roots cool, while other plants are just stood on top. Other base materials include grit and expanded clay particles. All of these must be clean and free from diseases.

SOME *plants, especially alpines, benefit from their pots being partly buried in clean gravel chippings. Other plants can just be stood on the surface. Moisture around the gravel rises and creates a desirable humid atmosphere around the plants.*

FIRM, *secure surfaces are needed for mist propagation units. The base has to support and contain moist sand as well as cuttings. A wooden framework, about 10cm/4in deep and lined with plastic, creates a waterproof base.*

SLATTED *staging is ideal for supporting plants that need a flow of dry air around their leaves. In winter, this is especially beneficial, when moisture lingering around foliage quickly encourages the spread of diseases.*

• <u>Mist-propagation units</u> – used to encourage cuttings to root quickly – need a firm, waterproof base. A wooden base and surround, covered with thick plastic sheeting, is an easy way to provide this. Access to water and electricity are essential: have the unit installed by a competent electrician and ensure all necessary safety devices are installed.

• <u>Temporary shelving</u> is often needed for boxes of seeds or seedlings in spring and early summer. Provide these by suspending long, narrow shelves from the glazing bars: if wooden, screw cables to the framework, but in aluminium greenhouses proprietary fittings are available. Take care when watering plants on the shelves that water does not drip on plants below. Also, remember that areas near the glass are the first to experience low-temperature falls during cold nights. It may be necessary to cover temporarily with sheets of newspaper at night. The insulative property of newspapers is high.

AMERICAN MILESTONE

The first record of a greenhouse in North America was in 1737, when Andrew Faneuil of Boston had one erected. In 1758, the construction of greenhouses was featured in a newspaper in New Amsterdam, later New York.

• <u>Tubular metal frameworks</u> with slatted or solid surfaces are ideal both as permanent or even as temporary fixtures.

• <u>Tiered staging</u> – usually permanent – is ideal for orchids, but ensure it is well constructed.

• <u>Hinged, wire-framed staging</u> is frequently available for fitting into aluminium houses, and has the advantage of being quickly collapsed when not required. Also, because it remains in the greenhouse there is not a storage problem. However, it does need to be thoroughly scrubbed and cleaned at the end of each growing season to ensure diseases are not present.

IN SPRING, *there is often a shortage of space. Narrow shelves can be suspended from wooden glazing bars, or from special brackets in aluminium constructions. When watering, take care moisture does not drip on plants below.*

MOVEABLE, *tubular staging is ideal where seeds of summer-flowering bedding plants are grown in spring and early summer, and the space is later needed for plants growing in pots or growing-bags at ground level in summer.*

TIERED, *wooden staging both displays plants so that they can be easily seen and allows a good circulation of air around them. Orchids especially benefit from this form of staging. Ensure each tier of the staging is firmly constructed.*

HEATING

§

FOR tropical and subtropical plants to be grown in temperate regions it is necessary to heat greenhouses during part or all of the year. Some plants can be grown in unheated greenhouses, but usually if the temperature falls dramatically and unexpectedly they will be damaged. Heating costs can be dramatically reduced by just using a greenhouse in spring and summer, perhaps to raise summer-flowering bedding plants and to grow tomatoes.

METHODS OF HEATING
These depend on the types of plants and if the structure is a greenhouse or conservatory.
• <u>Paraffin (kerosene) heaters</u> are relatively cheap to buy and inexpensive to operate. Also, by increasing the length of the wick the amount of heat created can be adjusted. But excessive amounts of wick create smoke.

Single and double burners – and in a range of sizes – are available. Some have hot-water pipes attached, so that warmth is given off along the pipes and from the exhausts at the ends.

When the heater is operating, oxygen is consumed and carbon dioxide given off. Therefore, unless the heater has a flue, ventilation is essential. Additionally, burning paraffin creates moisture: for every gallon of fuel burnt, a gallon of water is produced. An open ventilator will also allow this moisture to escape.
• <u>Bottle gas heaters</u> are easy to use, but like paraffin heaters increase the humidity. They are more expensive to operate than paraffin types and it is impossible to finely tune the amount of heat they give off – usually high or low. Also, it is necessary to have a spare gas bottle and there is little warning when a bottle is about to

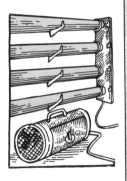

PARAFFIN *(kerosene) heaters are the simplest and cheapest way to heat greenhouses. There are several sizes and as long as wicks are properly trimmed and replaced each year they are safe and pleasant to use.*

BOTTLED *gas heaters are easy to use, but more expensive than paraffin. Also, it is necessary to have two gas bottles: one in use and the other as a spare. There is little warning when a bottle is becoming empty.*

ELECTRICITY *is easily controlled, but it must be installed properly. Tubular heaters are invariably fitted against walls, but fan-heaters are best positioned on the path and opposite the door. Avoid hot blasts.*

DEADLY DUO

Water and electricity are a lethal cocktail and must be kept separate. Water is sprayed to keep the atmosphere humid and unless electricity has been installed correctly there will be an accident that could be fatal.

Electrical standards dictate the installation of electricity into greenhouses and the need for water- and damp-proof cables and sockets. Safety devices include those that instantaneously cut off the power supply should there be a short in the circuit. Consult a specialist electrician.

finish. If this happens in the middle of a frosty night, the results could be disastrous.

• Electricity is ideal but expensive and therefore best installed in small greenhouses for limited periods. Temperatures can be controlled by thermostats, thereby reducing costs to a minimum. There are two types of heaters to choose from: tubular and fan.

Tubular heaters are invariably fixed to a wall and positioned about 25cm/10in above the ground. They produce a gentle flow of warm air. Ensure a 10–15cm/4–6in-wide gap is left between the back of the staging and the glass, so that heat can rise unimpeded from below.

Fan heaters create warmth and good air movement, which helps to combat fungus diseases. Do not use domestic fan heaters as they are unsafe in the high humidity of most greenhouses.

Both tubular and fan heaters produce dry heat, which may damage plants with tender leaves. Trays of water help to prevent this happening.

• Domestic heating systems can be extended to include conservatories and sunrooms. However, as the heating system is turned off at night, it may put plants at risk, especially where the construction is single-glazed. Double-glazing reduces the risk.

Clearly, the range of methods to heat greenhouses and conservatories is wide and the choice is influenced by many factors. The least expensive to install, as well as to operate, is a paraffin (kerosene) heater. It is also a flexible system as the heater can be easily moved to another greenhouse. Tubular electrical heaters, once installed are fixed, although fan types can be moved.

HEAT LOSS

The loss of warmth from a greenhouse is clearly influenced by the outside temperature. All surfaces of a greenhouse lose heat, whether glass, wood, metal or brickwork. Metal is more conductive than wood and therefore appears cooler and less cosy. Many wooden greenhouses have single-thickness brick walls at their bases, which lose warmth at about half the rate of glass. Heat loss also occurs through ill-fitting ventilators and doors, and so is avoidable in well maintained greenhouses

REDUCING HEAT LOSS

❖

Heating is a major cost factor in running a greenhouse and any way to reduce this is worth pursuing. Indeed, a wind-exposed situation or a frost-pocket could double the expense of heating a greenhouse during winter.

There are several ways to decrease the costs: correctly positioning the greenhouse, installing insulation, and carefully controlling the temperature.

POSITIONING

Orientate full-span greenhouses so that the ridge runs from east to west. This enables low, winter light to pass through the glass. Additionally, if tall plants are positioned on the side away from the sun they do not cast cooling shadows over others.

Avoid places shaded by buildings or trees, as well as overhanging trees that might drip rain on the greenhouse.

Position the door away from prevailing winds. Most doors in metal-framed greenhouses are on runners and slide across the opening, but wooden types are hinged, if possible, so that they open away from the prevailing wind.

A hedge on the windward side helps to reduce wind speed and therefore its cooling effect. Indeed, the benefit of a hedge can be felt up to a distance of thirty times its height. For instance, a hedge 2.4m/8ft high reduces the wind's speed by 75% at a point 4.5m/15ft from it. And at a distance of 12m/40ft the reduction is still as much as 65%.

Lean-to greenhouses require warm walls, especially to encourage the development of early-maturing crops.

INSULATION

Conserving heat is essential, especially if the greenhouse is used in winter. Bubble glazing, formed of three layers of plastic with air-bubbles between them, traps warmth within the greenhouse and is especially valuable for attaching to the coldest and most

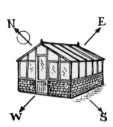

POSITION *a full-span (even span) greenhouse with its ridge from east to west. This allows maximum light to enter the structure, especially during winter. Position tall plants on the side opposite the sun, so that they do not cast shadows.*

LEAN-TO *greenhouses need warm, sun-facing walls to reduce heating costs and gain maximum light, especially in winter. Conservatories and sunrooms also need sunny situations against house walls, but sometimes this is not possible.*

Prevailing wind

AVOID *positions where trees cast shade. However, in exposed areas a windbreak or tree on the windward side helps to reduce heat loss. Position the door away from prevailing cold winds to prevent cool air rushing into the structure.*

exposed sides and roof. It is held in place by a range of fittings, including double-sided adhesive pads, drawing pins in wooden greenhouses and special clips in aluminium types.

Both white and green 'bubble' insulation is available: the green often makes the greenhouse too dark in winter, although if left in place in summer it creates useful shade. Other forms of insulative material include polythene sheets reinforced with wire mesh.

Large greenhouses can be made more economic to heat by partitioning them with these materials, but ensure they are firmly secured and cannot fall on top of a heater.

OPTIMUM TEMPERATURE

Clearly, the way to save money on heating is to have a 'cold house' and not provide any warmth – but this restricts the range of plants.

If the heating is limited to ensuring the temperature never falls below 7°C/45°F, this is called a 'cool house' and enables a wider range of plants to be grown.

Keeping the temperature at 16°C/61°F or more throughout

STOVE HOUSES

Greenhouses were first heated by stoves that were taken inside. Initially, no provision was made for hot, dangerous fumes to escape. Later, flues were installed but still plants and gardeners were at risk. Often the woodwork was set alight. However, the term 'stove' house is still used to describe very warm greenhouses.

---

the year enables tropical plants to be grown, but the cost is high.

An agreeable temperature compromise – and one that saves money – is just to heat the greenhouse in late winter and spring, when sowing seeds and raising young plants; and in summer to grow plants such as tomatoes that benefit from the protection afforded by a unheated greenhouse.

Using an electric or paraffin-heated propagator in late winter and early spring to encourage seed germination and the rooting of cuttings saves having to heat the entire greenhouse and reduces heating costs dramatically.

HEAT *loss can be dramatically reduced by insulating the insides of greenhouses. It is especially useful on sides exposed to cold, prevailing winds. Bubble-glazing – formed of three sheets of plastic – is especially effective.*

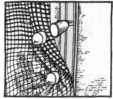

MANY *aluminium structures have channels in their glazing bars in which toggles can be inserted to secure insulation sheets, leaving a 2.5cm/1in gap between the material and glass. Ensure it reaches the ground and does not leave gaps.*

WARPED *ventilators and doors are a major source of heat loss. Inspect and adjust them in autumn. Avoid sealing them up in winter, as fresh air is often needed, especially when paraffin and bottle gas heaters are used to heat the structure.*

VENTILATION AND SHADING

❖

KEEPING a greenhouse, sunroom or conservatory at a temperature agreeable to plants during summer is essential. If temperatures are allowed to rise dramatically, plants soon lose moisture and eventually die. High light intensity through the glass also damages plants.

Temperatures in sunrooms and conservatories also rise quickly and, unless sufficient ventilators have been fitted, life for people as well as plants becomes unbearable.

FLOW OF AIR

Greenhouses and conservatories amply fitted with ventilators in their sides as well as roof areas have the opportunity of being well ventilated, even in summer.

On full-span greenhouses there must be ventilators on both sides, so that when cold winds are blowing only those on the lee side are opened. Cold draughts blowing on plants can cause the onset of diseases, especially in seedlings.

Preferably, roof ventilators should be fitted in every other pane of glass and in lean-to types continuously along the side. Hot air soon builds up in the roof area, and unless allowed to escape, damages plants, especially climbers with thin leaves.

Traditional wooden greenhouses with brick sides up to 75cm/2½ft high had ventilators low down that enabled an even better circulation of air.

In summer, doors can also be left open but if inquisitive birds are a problem, fit a wire-netting framework over the area. It may also be necessary to place netting over roof and side ventilators.

Automatic ventilators in both roof and side ventilators have enabled better control of summer temperatures throughout the day. Once the ventilator is installed, there is no operating cost.

Thermostatically-controlled electrically-operated extractor fans are effective and usually fitted in the gabled ends of greenhouses. Ensure louvres are fitted on the outside to prevent cold air blowing into the greenhouse.

DURING *summer, light intensity – even in temperate zones – can be too strong for many plants. The easiest, quickest and cheapest way to reduce this is to paint the glass with a proprietary shading liquid.*

ROLLER *blinds are costly to install but better than using a shading paint. They can be rolled up and down as the light intensity changes. This is advantageous during periods when the weather is unpredictable.*

FINE-MESHED *sheets of weather-resistant polypropylene netting, as well as polythene sheeting, are less expensive than roller blinds and can be draped quickly and easily over the sunny side of the greenhouse.*

SHADING

Strong light both damages plants and dramatically increases the temperature. The cheapest and easiest way to create shade is to paint the outside of the glass with a proprietary shading liquid. Do not paint the glazing bars and, if only light shading is needed, just coat the central two-thirds of each pane. Weather often removes the paint and during mid- to late summer fresh applications may possibly be needed.

Roller blinds, in varying widths, are better as they can be rolled up or down according to the weather. Some are made of canes, others slatted wood. Cheaper forms of roller blinds are formed from polypropylene netting, just flopped over the sunny side. Sheets of polythene can also be used.

Venetian blinds and roller blinds can be fitted to the insides of sunrooms and conservatories. Some of these are horizontal, while others are vertical and do not so easily collect dust.

VENTILATORS

Before buying a greenhouse, sunroom or conservatory, check that there are ventilators in the roof area that will enable hot air to easily escape.

On full-span greenhouses there must be roof ventilators on both sides, preferably every other pane of glass. Side ventilators are also essential. Ideally, lean-to greenhouses need continuous ventilators in the roof.

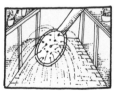

HUMIDITY *is essential to plants in high temperatures and strong sunlight. Regularly moisten the floor and between plants, but avoid dampening soft, hairy leaves, as well as flowers. They are soon damaged.*

AUTOMATIC *ventilators ensure temperatures within a greenhouse are constantly adjusted, even when you are not there. Both roof and side ventilators can be controlled by them and are certainly worth installing.*

EXTRACTOR *fans are often fitted into the gabled ends of the roof. Controlled by thermostats, they extract hot air from the roof area. Louvres on the outside prevent cold air blowing in on the plants.*

EQUIPMENT

❖

EVERY year, greenhouses are increasingly full of technical innovations, from thermostats and mist-propagation units to moisture meters and new methods of feeding plants. But it does not have to be complicated and it is quite easy to start with just a greenhouse, some means of heating it, a minimum and maximum registering thermometer and a few other pieces of equipment.

BASIC EQUIPMENT

Here are the basic pieces of equipment you will need:

• Plastic propagators help to raise new plants, whether seedlings or cuttings. The majority are heated by electricity, although a few rely on paraffin (kerosene) and therefore save the high cost of having electricity cables laid and installed. Other propagators are unheated, but create a humid atmosphere that benefits cuttings and a temperature – although not as uniform as in electrically-heated propagators – that is more even than in a seed-tray on its own. Also, the cover helps to prevent the compost rapidly drying.

• Sharp knives are essential when preparing cuttings: blunt ones leave ragged cuts that take longer to heal.

• Dibbers assist in transferring seedlings from the containers in which they were raised to seed-trays, where they are given more room. They are also useful when inserting cuttings into compost.

• Moisture testers are useful for assessing the amount of moisture in compost. Some have probes

PARAFFIN-HEATED *propagators are available and make propagation easier, even without electricity.*

INEXPENSIVE, *unheated propagators create humid environments with relatively even temperatures.*

SHARP *knives are essential when taking and trimming the bases of cuttings.*

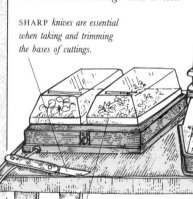

HEATED *propagators create warm, cosy environments for cuttings and seeds, encouraging rapid rooting and germination. They enable the greenhouse temperature to be lowered.*

SOIL *moisture testers take the guesswork out of assessing if compost is sufficiently moist. A probe is inserted into the compost and the amount of moisture it contains is indicated on a meter.*

DIBBERS *(like pencils) are needed to form holes in compost when seedlings are pricked out and spaced further apart.*

that are inserted into compost; the dial then indicates if further water is needed. However, repeated insertions of the probe damages the compost and roots. An alternative method is to insert label-like 'watering signals' into the compost – they change colour when water is needed.

• Mist-sprayers are essential for creating a humid atmosphere around plants, but take care not to moisten flowers or soft, hairy leaves. If damp, they decay and encourage the presence of diseases.

• Watering-cans with long spouts are essential in greenhouses. Gardening types are usually too cumbersome and with their short spouts are unable to reach plants at the backs of benches and stag-ing. However, garden types can be used to dampen floors. When selecting a long-spouted watering-can, choose one that is well balanced and has a long, curved handle that enables the can to be used whatever the amount of water in it. An oval watering rose is needed so that seedlings can be watered gently.

Both metal and plastic watering-cans are available.

• Thermometers of all kinds are available, but a minimum and maximum type is essential. Traditional, vertical types can be used, but more recent dial forms, where the readings are more easily reset, are clearer.

• Canes, string and metal clips are needed to support plants, firmly but not strangling them.

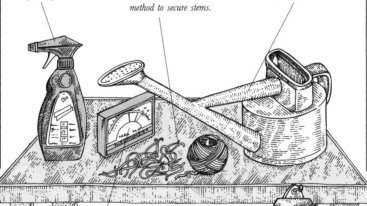

MIST-SPRAYERS *enable a humid atmosphere to be created around plants. Take care not to moisten flowers or soft, hairy leaves.*

SUPPORTING *plants is essential: plastic-covered metal rings that can be lightly squeezed around stems and supports are a quick method to secure stems.*

LONG-SPOUTED *watering-cans are essential to enable plants at the backs of staging to be watered without water splashing everywhere.*

MINIMUM AND MAXIMUM *thermometers are essential, enabling the temperature during the previous night to be recorded and a judgement to be made about the heat required.*

TRADITIONAL *minimum and maximum thermometers have been this design, using a magnet to reposition the high and low indicators. Later designs (at left), are simpler to read and reset.*

GETTING AUTOMATED

❖

REGULARLY watering plants has always been demanding, especially in summer when they may need a drink several times each day. This problem can be overcome in two ways and both are well within the abilities of most practical gardeners.

BOTTLE RESERVOIR

This system does not need a mains water supply and therefore is suitable in all greenhouses.

Invert and secure a refillable bottle of water and, using flexible piping, conduct water into a waterproof plastic tray. The neck of the bottle needs to be level with the surface of a strip of capillary matting laid in the tray's base. By adjusting the height of the reservoir, the level of water can be raised and lowered. If the reservoir has an open top, water will pass out steadily. However, if it is formed of a closed bottle, a further pipe needs to be fitted to pre-

vent a vacuum forming in the bottle's top and the flow of water being stopped.

Stand pots on top of the capillary matting. Plastic pots do not have crocks (broken pieces pieces of clay pot) placed in their bases and therefore water readily passes from the matting to the compost. Clay pots, however, are usually crocked and therefore the compost will not readily absorb water. Insert a wick into the base of each pot so that it acts as a channel for the water from the sand.

To reduce evaporation from the capillary matting, place a plastic sheet over it, with holes cut out for the pots. Alternatively, use a 12–18mm/^{1}/$_2$–^{3}/$_4$in layer of sand.

TRICKLE IRRIGATION

Once operating, this system can be left in operation without any attention for several days. Water is usually supplied by mains water and a ballock used to ensure the

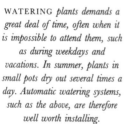

WATERING *plants demands a great deal of time, often when it is impossible to attend them, such as during weekdays and vacations. In summer, plants in small pots dry out several times a day. Automatic watering systems, such as the above, are therefore well worth installing.*

THIS *watering system provides each plant with a regular drip of water. The amount of water each plant receives is easily controlled by nozzles. A series of small-bore, flexible pipes – known as spaghetti piping – conduct the water. The supply of water can be from the mains or a tank.*

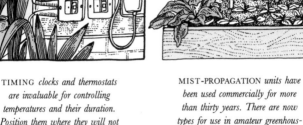

TIMING *clocks and thermostats
are invaluable for controlling
temperatures and their duration.
Position them where they will not
be sprayed with water, as well as
out of strong, direct sunlight.*

MIST-PROPAGATION *units have
been used commercially for more
than thirty years. There are now
types for use in amateur greenhouses. They need an electrical supply,
as well as mains water.*

water-level remains constant.
Alternatively, use a large plastic
tank as a water reservoir.
Unfortunately, this does not provide constant water pressure and
the flow of water alters. Use tub-
ing to direct water into the top of
each pot, its flow controlled by
nozzles. Initially, regular attention
is needed to ensure the right
amount of water is reaching each
plant. Avoid waterlogging plants.

MIST-PROPAGATION UNITS

At one time, these were only
available to commercial nurserymen, but now amateur types are
available. They create a mist of
water over cuttings, keeping them
cool and reducing the need for
them to absorb moisture before
new roots are formed.

THERMOSTATS AND TIMERS

The range of electrical equipment
is wide and includes thermostats
to control temperatures.
Combined with timing devices,
electrical equipment can be controlled to come on and off – and
to desired temperatures – at the
touch of a switch.

SOLAR POWER!

In 1826, The Gardener's
Magazine *revealed details of a
scheme to store warm water in
underground cisterns. Water was
to be heated by the sun's rays
warming a hollow ball. It was
anticipated that the water could
later be used to heat
greenhouses.*

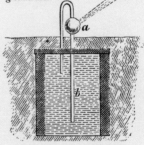

*At about the same time, John
Loudon, a visionary and
distinguished author, outlined a
way to extract heat from the
earth's crust through bore holes,
an idea still pursued in the late
twentieth century.*

POTS AND
OTHER CONTAINERS

CONTAINERS of all kinds are used to create homes for plants in greenhouses. Some provide temporary situations for cuttings or seeds, while others, such as pots, remain with plants until larger ones are needed.

Clay pots are the traditional homes for plants in greenhouses, but during recent decades plastic types have gained popularity. However, both types grow healthy plants, and each have advantages and disadvantages.

CLAY POTS
• Break easily when dropped.
• Heavier than plastic types and create firm bases for large plants.
• More difficult to clean than plastic types.
• If dry, they must be soaked in water for twenty-four hours before use. If not, they absorb moisture from the compost. This reduces the amount available for plants.

• Have a natural colour and harmonize with plants.
• Have a porous nature and allow damaging salts from some fertilizers to escape.
• Encourage potting composts to remain cool in summer and warm in winter.
• Are usually used in conjunction with loam-based composts.

PLASTIC POTS
• Light and easy to handle, especially for disabled gardeners.
• Become brittle with age, especially after being stored at low temperatures.
• Are not porous and therefore do not allow damaging salts in the compost to escape.
• Are usually used in conjunction with peat-based composts.
• Available in a wide colour range and are well suited to harmonize in modern settings.
• Do not need to have broken pieces of pots in their bases, unlike clay pots.

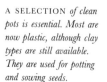

A SELECTION *of clean pots is essential. Most are now plastic, although clay types are still available. They are used for potting and sowing seeds.*

SOME *seed-trays are divided into sections so that each seedling is given the same amount of space. Later, it makes transplanting into a garden much easier.*

TRADITIONAL *wooden seed boxes have been replaced by plastic seed-trays, which are easily cleaned and stored. They are available in two basic sizes.*

SEED-TRAYS

Plastic seed-trays are ideal for raising seeds and for transferring seedlings into. Full-sized seed-trays measure about 35cm x 23cm x 5cm/14in x 9in x 2in; mini ones are 23cm x 18cm x 5cm/9in x 7in x 2in. There must be several drainage holes in their bases to enable excess moisture to escape.

SECTIONED SEED-TRAYS

Seed-trays are now frequently divided into sections, enabling individual cuttings or seedlings to be put in each hole. Later, when plants are transplanted, a special device is often used to force out the plants gently but firmly from their individual squares.

PEAT POTS

These are formed of sphagnum moss peat – plus fertilizers – compressed into the form of pots. Individual seedlings are grown in them and later, when the whole pot is planted into a garden, do not suffer any shock.

They range in size and shape: 36mm/1¹/₂in and 6cm/2¹/₂in square, or about 6cm/2¹/₂in round. They are sold in packs.

Because the compressed peat is exposed to the air, careful watering is needed when growing plants in them to ensure they do not become dry.

LARGE PLASTIC TRAYS

These are invaluable for housing several pots or seed-trays. Then, rather than moving them individually, they can be moved as a group. This prevents seed-trays twisting and the compost becoming disturbed and loosened.

Large trays are also useful when propagating houseplants by layering runners; a mother plant is placed in the centre and stems pregged into small pots, also on it.

GROWING-BAGS

These were originally introduced to make tomato growing easier, especially in soils contaminated with diseases. Today, they are used in greenhouses – as well as on patios – for a wide range of plants, including vegetables, herbs and ornamental plants, especially those with an ephemeral nature and grown solely for their bright summer colours.

Basically, they are strong, plastic bags filled with a peat-based compost combined with fertilizers. Before using a bag, shake to loosen the compost, which may have become compacted.

Use a sharp knife or scissors to cut along the dotted lines on the top of the bag and tuck the flaps under to form a strong lip to the sides.

Usually, the compost is adequately moist but if dry, soak it thoroughly. Allow excess moisture to drain before setting plants in it.

Bags can be reused for growing flowers on a patio during the following year, but freshen up the compost with a general fertilizer.

An unusual way to reuse these bags is to place them along the edges of flat roofs and garages and fill them with plants.

COMPOSTS

❖

Garden soil is not suitable for growing plants in pots and boxes as it is variable in quality, often badly drained and may contain weed seeds, pests and diseases. Specially-prepared composts are needed and basically there are two types to choose from: loam-based and peat-based.

LOAM-BASED COMPOSTS

These are formed of sterilized loam, sharp sand and peat, with the addition of ground chalk and fertilizers. There are two types: one in which seeds are sown and the other for potting up plants. Additionally, the potting type is available in three strengths of fertilizers to suit plants throughout their lives.

They are heavier than peat-based types and therefore give more stability to large plants. Drying out is less rapid than with peat types and they have a greater reserve of plant foods.

PEAT-BASED COMPOSTS

Also known as loamless composts, these are newer. Formed basically of granulated peat, they are sold in several forms, for seed-sowing or potting. Some are multi-purpose.

They are more uniform than loam-based types, suitable for most plants and relatively light to use and carry home. Storage is easy as bags can be re-sealed and placed in a cool, dry place.

Plants growing in them need to be fed at an earlier stage than in loam-based types, and are more difficult to re-moisten if watering is neglected.

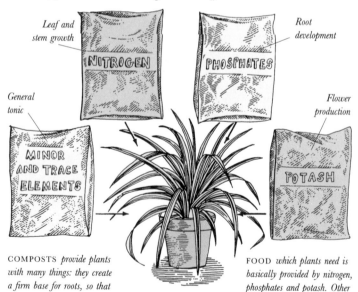

Leaf and stem growth — NITROGEN

Root development — PHOSPHATES

General tonic — MINOR AND TRACE ELEMENTS

Flower production — POTASH

COMPOSTS *provide plants with many things: they create a firm base for roots, so that they are able to support stems and leaves. They also provide air and moisture for roots.*

A BALANCED *diet of food is also essential: either initially provided in the compost or added later.*

FOOD *which plants need is basically provided by nitrogen, phosphates and potash. Other nutrients are needed in much smaller amounts, and are usually present in the compost initially.*

PLANT FOODS

❖

THERE are many chemicals plants require for healthy growth; some are major, others only needed in small amounts and therefore known as minor or trace elements. The three major ones are nitrogen, phosphorus (phosphates) and potassium (potash).

NITROGEN
This is basically leaf-making; it encourages the growth of stems.
• Too much encourages sappy, luxuriant growth prone to attack from pests and diseases. Stems become floppy and the quality and number of flowers is reduced. Leaves also become dark green and flowering is delayed.
• Too little creates small plants, and leaves assume yellowish-green tints. Old leaves become yellow.

PHOSPHATE
Vital for the development of roots.
• Too much encourages yellowish-green leaves and young stems become mature quickly. Shoots become rigid and maturity is hastened.
• Too little creates small leaves with purple tinting on a dark green background.

POTASH
Encourages balanced growth and is vital for the development of fruits and a plant's ability to survive adverse conditions.
• Too much causes growth to harden and delays flower development.
• Too little causes stunted growth and plants susceptible to low temperature damage. Old leaves become mottled.

ALL plants need a balanced diet of fertilizers to encourage healthy growth. Here are the results of a few deficiencies, but symptoms vary between species: the ones here relate to a tomato plant.

YOUNG *leaves are the first to reveal iron deficiency: initially they are yellowish-green; later white.*

SMALL *leaves with purple shading on a dark green background indicate phosphate deficiency. Leaves become cupped.*

YELLOW *areas between veins on lower leaves indicate a lack of magnesium. Later, they become brown.*

PALE *green or yellowish leaves indicate a shortage of nitrogen, as does thin, leggy and weak growth.*

BROWN *leaf edges that curl upwards are symptoms of potash deficiency. It is accompanied by poor flowering and fruiting.*

PLANT *foods are mainly absorbed by roots, but it is also possible to apply some by spraying in a weak solution on leaves. This is known as foliar feeding.*

WATERING

❖

WATER is essential to plants, but either too much or too little causes death. Plants absorb water through their roots and give it off through small, hole-like pores, known as *stoma*, mainly on the undersides of leaves. This continuous cycle of water keeps plants cool, firm and upright, as well as transporting foods from the soil to the leaves.

JUDGING WHEN WATER IS NEEDED

This is a skill not easily acquired and usually gained only after years of experience, although in recent years specialized equipment has been introduced to take the guesswork out of this task.

• The surface of compost indicates when water is needed: when dry it is pale and crumbly, but dark if wet. This is one of the best methods, as it does not disturb or compress the compost.

• Rubbing a finger or thumb on the compost is a popular method: if damp, no water is needed. However, repeated pressings eventually damage the compost.

• Tapping the side of a pot with a cotton reel (bobbin) on the end of a short cane is a traditional method, but only works on clay pots. If the knock gives a dull note, no water is needed; if a ringing tone, moisture is needed.

• Moisture-indicator strips – also known as watering signals – inserted into compost change colour when water is needed.

• Moisture-meters indicate precisely when water is needed, but repeated insertions of a probe into compost is eventually destructive.

APPLYING WATER

Most plants in pots are watered 'over the rim'. This means that a watering-can is used to fill up the gap between the compost and the rim. If water runs out quickly, water it again. The first watering expands the compost, the next thoroughly soaks it.

Soft and hairy-leaved plants are soon damaged by water on their leaves. Therefore, stand their pots in a bowl of water until moisture seeps to the surface, then remove and allow to drain.

STORE *composts and fertilizers in a cool, dry shed. Preferably, stand them on a slatted wooden framework in case the floor is damp or becomes wet.*

ENVIRONMENTALLY-FRIENDLY COMPOSTS

The continued taking of peat from peat-bogs has decimated the natural environment and destroyed the homes of many plants, birds and insects. Therefore, alternatives have been sought. Some composts – now on the market – are formed from the outer husks of coconuts and said to be as good, if not better, than peat types.

FEEDING PLANTS

❖

ONCE plants have exhausted the food in compost, they need further nourishment. Regular feeding during a plant's growing period makes a remarkable difference. Feed both foliage and summer-flowering greenhouse plants from early spring to late summer at ten to fourteen-day intervals. Winter-flowering types, however, are fed at the same intervals during the period they remain in flower. Never feed plants when they are dormant, as they are unable to use the food.

TOPDRESSING

Large plants in greenhouses, sunrooms and conservatories are frequently too big to be repotted. Topdress them in spring instead. Allow the compost to dry slightly and then scrape away the top 2.5cm/1in. For very large plants, perhaps in tubs in a large conservatory, increase this to 36mm/1½in. Replace this with fresh potting compost, leaving a 12–18mm/½–¾in gap between the compost and rim to allow the plant to be properly watered.

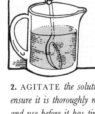

1. MOST PLANTS *are fed by diluting a proprietary liquid fertilizer in water. Adhere to the manufacturer's instructions about the concentration.*

2. AGITATE *the solution to ensure it is thoroughly mixed and use before it has time to settle. If the mixture is too strong, it will damage the roots of the plant.*

3. DO NOT *apply the liquid to dry compost: it will either damage roots or run out of the gap between the soil-ball and pot. Thoroughly water the compost first.*

ANOTHER *way is to push pills into the compost, again about 12mm/½in from the edge. Some devices enable pills to be inserted into the compost without having to dirty your hands.*

AN ALTERNATIVE *to liquid feeding is to use feeding sticks pushed into the compost, about 12mm/½in from the pot's side. It is quick and easy and provides food over a long period.*

FERTILIZER *powders are sometimes used: they are dusted evenly on the compost's surface and watered in. They are best used on plants growing in large pots.*

CUTTINGS

❖

ANY plants can be easily increased in greenhouses by taking cuttings and inserting them in equal parts moist peat and sharp sand. The range of cuttings is wide and includes soft-wood cuttings, leaf cuttings, leaf-petiole cuttings and leaf-stem cuttings. Here are two popular methods.

LEAF-STEM CUTTINGS

These are mainly used to increase ivies, which have long stems peppered with leaves.

Select a healthy, relatively young stem and cut slightly above each leaf. This produces a series of individual leaves, each with a stem attached. Trim these stems to about 36mm/1¹/₂in long. For ivies with large leaves, increase this to 5cm/2in.

Fill and firm a pot with equal parts moist peat and sharp sand, then insert the cuttings so that each leaf is just above the compost. Do not insert cuttings closer than 12mm/¹/₂in to the pot's edge, as this is where the compost first becomes dry if watering is inadvertently forgotten.

Water the cuttings, allowing excess to drain and moisture to evaporate from the leaves. Then, insert four or five thin canes around the edge and cover with a plastic bag, securing it around the pot with an elastic band. When shoots develop from leaf joints, remove the bag, lower the temperature and transfer (pot up) the cuttings into other pots, putting three or five in each one. This produces attractive plants more readily than just using a single cutting in each pot. Place in light shade until established and growing strongly.

1. IVIES *can be easily increased by cutting healthy stems to form several cuttings. Cut a stem from a mother plant, using a sharp knife to form the cuttings. Sever just above leaf-joints, so that each cutting is formed of a leaf and 36mm/ 1¹/₂in-long piece of stem.*

2. FILL AND FIRM *a pot with equal parts moist peat and sharp sand. Use a dibber to form holes, then insert and firm the stem so that the leaf is above the compost.*

3. WATER *the compost. Insert thin canes around the edge and cover with a plastic bag. Seal with an elastic band. Remove when the cuttings develop young shoots.*

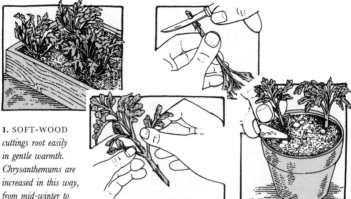

1. SOFT-WOOD *cuttings root easily in gentle warmth. Chrysanthemums are increased in this way, from mid-winter to late spring, depending on their types. Water the mother plant the day before taking the cuttings. Sever the shoots at their bases.*

2. PREPARE *each cutting carefully. Remove the lower leaves (lower drawing), then trim the base of each cutting (top) just below a leaf joint.*

3. INSERT *and firm four or five cuttings into a 7.5cm/ 3in-wide pot, setting them about 2.5cm/1in deep. Water them gently.*

INCREASING CHRYSANTHEMUMS

Soft-wood cuttings are each formed of a shoot tip and a few leaves. They are used to increase many plants, such as chrysanthemums and dahlias.

Each autumn, chrysanthemums are cut down to soil level and their roots put in boxes with soil packed around them. The roots are known as stools. They are overwintered in a frost-proof shed or greenhouse and during winter or early spring watered and given gentle warmth to encouraged the development of young shoots.

The precise time when chrysanthemum cuttings are taken and rooted depends on their type: large-flowered greenhouse types are rooted in mid- and late winter; early-flowering greenhouse types in mid-spring; and late-flowering greenhouse types in late spring or early summer. Outdoor varieties are propagated in early spring.

Use a sharp knife to sever cuttings from the stools. They should be short-jointed, 5–6.5cm/

2–2^1/$_2$in long and trimmed just below a leaf joint. Remove the lower leaves and put their bases in hormone rooting-powder.

Insert them into pots filled and firmed with equal parts moist peat and sharp sand. Insert about five cuttings in a 7.5cm/3in pot, ensuring they are positioned slightly in from the pot's side. Firm them and lightly water the compost to settle it around the bases of the cuttings.

Allow excess moisture to drain from the compost – and all moisture to evaporate from the leaves – then insert small canes in the compost and cover with a plastic bag. Secure the bag around the pot's base with an elastic band.

Place in gentle warmth and light shade. Inspect the compost regularly and water as necessary. When young shoots develop, remove the plastic bag. Later, pot up into individual pots containing potting compost. Water and place in gentle warmth and light shade until established. Later, they are potted up into individual pots.

FLOWERS TO
RAISE FROM SEEDS

❖

MANY of the brightest and best-known flowering plants for decorating homes can be raised from seeds sown in greenhouses. They can also be raised and displayed in sunrooms and conservatories. Here is a selection of some of the popular ones.

• *Cyclamen persicum* (Florist's Cyclamen) is best known for brightening late summer to mid-winter with swept-back flowers on long stalks, although they do bloom earlier. Colour range: white, red, pink or purple. Plants are 15–23cm/6–9in high and 15–25cm/6–10in wide.

Sow seeds 6mm/¹⁄₄in deep in 13–18°C/55–64°F during mid- to late summer for flowering twelve to eighteen months later. Germination takes approximately three weeks.

• *Senecio cruentus* (Cineraria and earlier known as *Cineraria cruenta*) creates large heads of daisy-like flowers from early winter to early summer in colours including white, blue, purple, pink and red. Several different strains are available in a range of sizes, but the most popular is the 'Grandiflora' type at 30–45cm/12–18in high and 30–38cm/12–15in wide.

1. Cyclamen persicum *(Florist's Cyclamen) is widely seen in flower from late summer to mid-winter.*

2. Senecio cruentus *(Cineraria) develops dome-like heads from early winter to early summer.*

3. Kalanchoe blossfeldiana *(Flaming Katy) ordinarily flowers from late winter to late spring.*

4. Calceolaria x herbeohybrida *(Slipper Flower) creates pouch-like flowers.*

5. Primula obconica *(Poison Primrose) flowers from early winter to spring.*

6. Primula sinensis *(Chinese Primrose) flowers from early winter to spring.*

Sow seeds 3mm/$\frac{1}{8}$in deep in 13°C/55°F during late spring and early summer. Germination takes ten to fourteen days.

• *Kalanchoë blossfeldiana* (Flaming Katy) ordinarily flowers from late winter to late spring, but commercial horticulturalists are able to manipulate periods of light and darkness to produce flowering plants throughout the year. In a home greenhouse this is difficult, and plants are grown to flower at their normal times. Flowers are usually red, but orange and yellow types are available. Sow seeds slightly less than 3mm/$\frac{1}{8}$in deep and place in 21°C/70°F in early spring to produce plants that flower during the following year. Germination then takes two to three weeks.

• *Calceolaria x herbeohybrida* (Slipper Flower) is spectacular, with pouch-shaped flowers, spotted or blotched, in shades of yellow, orange and red, from late spring to mid-summer. Sow seeds on the surface of compost (just pressing them in and not covering) during mid-summer. Place in 16–20°C/61–68°F. Germination takes two to three weeks.

• *Primula obconica* (Poison Primrose) develops flowers from early winter to late spring. Sow seeds in early spring, lightly covering them, and place in 16°C/61°F. Germination takes ten to twenty-one days.

• *Primula malacoides* (Fairy Primrose) develops star-like, lightly-fragrant flowers from early winter to early spring. Sow seeds in exactly the same way as recommended for *P. obconica*.

• *Primula sinensis* (Chinese Primrose) develops whorls of flowers, each up to 36mm/1$\frac{1}{2}$in wide, from early winter to early spring. Sow seeds in the same way as for *P. obconica*.

SOWING CACTI

Children love sowing cacti seeds and watching them develop into a wide range of shapes and sizes. They are easy to raise from seeds and can be sown indoors on a warm window sill.

Several mixtures of seeds are offered by seed companies, such as easily raised and common types, rare and sought-after species, specific cacti such as Old Man Cacti (Cephalocereus senilis) *and quick-growing columnar types.*

Fill the base of a wide pot with clean, coarse drainage material, then compost. Sprinkle sharp sand on it to create extra drainage. Sprinkle seeds lightly and evenly evenly over the surface, but not within 12mm/$\frac{1}{2}$in of the sides. Do not cover them. Place the pot in a bowl of water; remove when moisture seeps to the surface. Allow to drain then cover with a plastic dome or bag. A temperature of about 21°C/70°F is desirable.

Some seeds germinate within a few days, others much later. Remove the covering after germination and eventually transfer the seedlings to other pots and containers.

SOWING SEEDS

❖

SEEDS are nature's way of creating a large number of new plants at one time. Usually, however, only the strongest and most fortunate seeds germinate.

In greenhouses, sunrooms and conservatories it is easy to provide the essentials for germination: moisture, air and warmth. Additionally, most seeds need darkness, but a few require light.

SOWING SEEDS

The essentials for germination are provided by moisture-retentive but well-drained compost and gentle warmth. Both loam-based and peat-based composts have forms ideal for sowing seeds in, while a suitable temperature is provided by a greenhouses. Alternatively, propagation cases heated by electricity or paraffin (kerosene) create the necessary warmth.

The general method of sowing seeds is detailed below, but fine seeds can be more easily – and certainly more evenly – sown by first mixing them with twice the amount of dry silver sand.

After they are sown, most seeds need darkness and this is provided by placing a few sheets of newspaper over the plastic lid or sheet of glass covering them. It also helps to retain warmth and prevent temperature fluctuations.

As soon as seeds germinate, remove the paper to prevent the seedlings being drawn up and weakened. When most of the seeds have germinated, also remove the plastic or glass covering. First remove it partly, and then only during the day. Later, remove at night.

Always avoid cold draughts blowing on seedlings, as this encourages the onset of diseases. Once seeds have germinated and seedlings are growing strongly it is best to water them from above with a fine-rosed can. Do this in the morning, so that leaves and stems are dry by evening when the temperature falls slightly.

At this stage, the seedlings need fresh air to enable them to grow strongly. Later, they are pricked out and given more space.

1. WHEN *preparing to sow seeds, first fill a seed-tray with compost and firm it evenly, especially around the edges. Loose compost dries out extremely quickly and later could cause the deaths of seedlings if watering is neglected.*

2. USE *a straight-edged piece of wood to level the compost with the edges of the seed-tray. Then, use a presser (a piece of wood about 15cm/6in by 10cm/4in) to firm the surface to about 12mm/¹/2in below the edge.*

3. TIP *seeds in a piece of stiff paper folded into a V-shape. Then, lightly tap its edge so that seeds fall evenly and thinly over the surface. Do not sow within 12mm/¹/2in of the tray's edges, as this is where compost first becomes dry.*

TEMPERATURES

Because we attempt to germinate seeds of plants native to many temperate, tropical and subtropical regions, it is not surprising that the range of temperatures they need varies widely. Mostly, however, a daytime temperature of 18–24°C/64–75°F is suitable, with a drop at night to about 13°C/55°F. After germination, provide a day temperature of about 13–16°C/55–61°F and a position out of direct sunlight.

If you do not have a greenhouse – or enough spare space in it during spring – seed-trays can initially be placed above central-heating boilers or in airing cupboards. But as soon as seeds germinate, move the seed-tray into better light. Window sills are also suitable, but avoid those in strong light. Too high temperatures soon 'fry' and kill seedlings, whereas lower temperatures in lightly-shaded positions might take longer to encourage germination but in the long term are more successful.

Venetian blinds or net curtains help to diffuse strong sunlight, thereby improving the position.

ALTERNATIVE COVER

In earlier years, before plastic seed-trays when omly wooden seed-boxes were available, seeds were covered with a sheet of glass and then a couple of layers of newspaper. This is still an excellent method, but each morning wipe away condensation from the underside of the glass, as well as turning it over. If left, moisture drips on the seeds and compost, encouraging the presence of diseases. Moisture also needs to be removed from the insides of plastic domes. Take care, when using glass, not to leave it where children or pets are likely to touch it.

4. USE *a horticultural sieve to lightly cover the seeds to between three and four times their thickness. Some seeds, however, are just scattered on the surface and not covered. Domestic sieves can also be used to cover the seeds, but clog if the compost is moist.*

5. WATER *the compost by standing the seed-tray in a bowl with about 36mm/1^1/2in of water in it. When moisture seeps to the surface, remove and allow excess to drain. Do not water from above, as this scatters the seeds over the surface.*

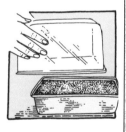

6. COVER *the seed-tray with a clear plastic dome to prevent moisture evaporating from the compost and to maintain an even temperature. Most seeds germinate in darkness, so cover the tray with a sheet of newspaper.*

PRICKING OUT SEEDLINGS

❖

AS SOON as seedlings are large enough to handle they must be transferred to wider spacings in other seed-trays. This is known as pricking out. If seedlings are left in the seed-tray they become congested, weak and spindly, a state from which they will not recover. Additionally, congested seedlings are more susceptible to diseases than those with a good air circulation around them.

PRICKING OUT

Transplanting any plant is a delicate operation, but the younger they are the more successful it is. After seeds germinate, slowly acclimatize the seedlings to lower temperatures so that they are growing sturdily. Then, as soon as they are large enough to handle move them to wider spacings.

The day before pricking out, water the seedlings in their seed-tray, so that the compost is thoroughly moist. Use a small fork (sometimes sold with dibbers) to lift out a cluster of seedlings. Place them on moist newspaper or hessian to prevent their roots drying. Push compost around the roots of disturbed seedlings in the seed-tray to prevent them becoming dry and damaged.

Fill and firm potting compost in a clean seed-tray so that its surface is 12mm/^{1}/2in below the rim. Use a clean dibber to make holes in the compost, spacing them about 36mm/1^1/2in apart and no closer than 12mm/^{1}/2in to the container's sides. This safeguards the seedlings if watering is neglected and the compost becomes dry.

Hold each seedling by a leaf and position its roots in a hole, so it is at the same depth as before. Ensure the roots are not twisted and then use the dibber to firm compost around them. Never hold a seedling by its stem as it is then soon damaged.

When the seed-tray is full, gently tap its sides to level loose compost on the surface. This prevents water later collecting in puddles on the surface. Stand the

1. AS *soon as seedlings fill their seed-tray they must be given more space. This is called 'pricking out' and involves moving seedlings carefully and individually into further seed-trays containing potting compost.*

2. WATER *the seedlings thoroughly but gently, then the following day use a small fork to lift up a cluster of them. Place them on a piece of damp newspaper or hessian to prevent their roots drying.*

3. PREPARE *a seed-tray in the same manner as when sowing seeds – filling and levelling to 12mm/^{1}/2in below the rim. Use a dibber to form holes about 36mm/ 1^1/2in apart, the outer ones 12mm/^{1}/2in from the sides.*

seed-tray on a level, well-drained surface, and water lightly but thoroughly from above with a fine-rosed watering-can. Allow excess water to drain before placing the seed-tray on a shelf in a greenhouse. And remember to insert a label into the compost, giving the date and also the name of the plants.

Place the seedlings in a warm and lightly-shaded position until established and growing strongly. As they develop and their leaves grow, ensure that moisture falling on them when the compost is watered has sufficient time to dry before nightfall.

If you have seedlings to spare, offer them to neighbours or friends, who might be able to make an exchange of other plants.

INDIVIDUAL HOLES

Proprietary trays in which there are individual square or round holes are an alternative to normal seed-trays. A seedling is pricked out into each hole, ensuring equal spacing. The holes or squares range from 36mm/1in wide to just under 6mm/2$\frac{1}{2}$in and therefore can accommodate a wide size range of seedlings.

GREENHOUSE OR CONSERVATORY

Greenhouse and conservatory were originally synonymous terms and widely used for glass structures used to house and conserve 'greens' and 'evergreens' from warm climates. The term greenhouse was first coined during the late 1600s by John Evelyn, English garden designer, writer and translator of books.

Nowadays, a greenhouse tends to be a place where the practicalities of gardening are performed: seeds sown, cuttings rooted and plants nurtured until large enough to be taken indoors or planted into a garden. Glasshouse is a term which is mainly reserved for commercial greenhouses.

Conservatories now tend to be places as much for relaxation as growing plants, although there is no doubt plants introduce life to a structure that otherwise appears barren Sunrooms are an American innovation and very much assume the functions of conservatories.

4. HOLD *each seedling by a leaf and position it in a hole, at about the same depth as before and with its roots well spread out. Carefully lever compost around them, taking care not to crush the stem.*

5. WHEN *the seed-tray is full of seedlings, gently tap its edges to level loose surface compost. Water seedlings from above to settle compost around their roots. Allow excess water to drain from the seed tray.*

6. PLACE *the seed-tray in gentle warmth and light shade until the seedlings are established. Keep the compost moist, but not waterlogged, and when the plants touch each other transfer them into small pots.*

POTTING UP

❖

Whe young plants growing in seed-trays fill their container with leaves and roots, transfer them to individual pots. If left, they become stunted, with their foliage drawn and etiolated. From this state, plants seldom recover and even if given ideal conditions, do not develop into healthy plants.

Because of the continued necessity to move plants from one container to another – to give them more space, light and air – it may appear to be easier to put them in large containers at an early stage. However, this is not so: small seedlings in large containers are surrounded by soil which remains cold and wet because of the lack of root activity in it. Additionally, it makes keeping the correct moisture content very difficult and usually it becomes excessively wet.

Another factor is the amount of space initially needed if plants are immediately put in large pots. During spring, space is usually at a premium in greenhouses and there is none to be wasted.

MOIST COMPOST

Always water plants the day before transferring them into pots. Plants with dry roots receive a check to their growth; however, they should not be swamped with water either.

Commercial nurserymen remove plants from boxes by knocking an end and side on the ground and then, with sudden movement, raising the seed-tray and tossing the plants forward so that they remain in a block. The matted roots hold the compost together. However, risking this action on cherished plants is rash and therefore the safest way for home gardeners to remove plants is to use a fork or small trowel.

Use clean, dry pots and fill the base of one with compost. Position a plant in it to ensure that when potted it will be slightly lower than before. The old soil-level can be seen on the stem. Setting the plant slightly lower than before allows for the later settlement of compost when watered.

1. WHEN *young plants that previously were pricked out into seed-trays are congested they must be transferred into small pots or planted into a garden. The day before moving them into pots (potting up) thoroughly water the compost.*

2. SHARPLY *tap the sides of the seed-tray several times to loosen the compost and prevent it adhering to the container. Then, use a fork or small trowel to lift out a plant, taking care not to damage its roots, especially the fine ones.*

3. FILL *a clean pot's base with potting compost, so that when potted the plant will be slightly lower than before. This allows for subsequent settlement of the compost when watering after potting is completed. Add compost, as needed.*

Still holding the plant, dribble compost around and over the roots, then firming with finger tips to fractionally less than 12mm/ ¹/₂in below the pot's rim.

Water the compost to settle it around the roots, then place the plant in a warm, lightly-shaded position. When growth resumes, decrease the temperature and give more light.

As growth progresses, space plants further apart, so that their leaves are not touching each other. Keep the compost moist but not waterlogged.

SOFT OR HARD POTTING?

Earlier, the technique of repotting plants – especially when potting greenhouse chrysanthemums into large pots – was to ram as much soil-based compost as possible into the pot. This was to ensure that the maximum amount of food was initially given to a plant, as well as to hold it secure and able to support stems up to 1.5m/5ft high. Nowadays, soft-potting is performed, where only moderate firming is necessary.

POTTING TIME

The art and timing of potting up or repotting established plants in pots has been well known to gardeners for many centuries. In the early 1800s, Sir Joseph Paxton, the English gardener and architect (who designed the Crystal Palace which housed the Great Exhibition of 1851) said: "It is a standing rule with experienced horticulturalists that no plant should be allowed a larger pot till the one in which it is growing is filled with fibrous roots."

This axiom is still right and applies in all places, although in the tropics it is advantageous if plants are repotted when commencing active growth, which is usually at the beginning of the monsoon rains. Orchids are also repotted when growth begins: or otherwise when their flowering season is over.

4. POSITION *the plant on the compost and gently hold its stem in the pot's centre. Trickle potting compost around the roots, taking care not to damage the stem – young plants are easily damaged and may not fully recover.*

5. USE *the tips of fingers to firm compost over and around the roots, so that its surface is about 12mm/ ¹/₂in below the rim. Water the compost from above to settle it around the roots. Place in gentle warmth and light shade.*

6. WHEN *growth resumes, lower the temperature and position in better light. Initially, stand the pots close together: this saves space and reduces moisture loss from the compost. As plants develop, remember to space them further apart.*

REPOTTING

❖

WHEN plants fill their pots with roots they must be repotted to prevent growth eventually becoming stunted. It is essential that plants are progressively moved in only small stages and not given too much fresh compost at one time. If this happens, it is difficult to keep the moisture content in the compost at the correct level, especially in winter when plants are not growing rapidly.

SELECTING A POT

The size of the new pot will depend on that of the existing one. For example, the following changes are about right: move a plant in a 6cm/2$\frac{1}{2}$in pot into a 8cm/3$\frac{1}{2}$in one. Then, repot it into a 13cm/5in pot and later into a 18cm/7in one. Eventually, a change into a 25cm/10in pot might be needed for a very large plant in a conservatory or sunroom such as a palm.

WATERING SPACE

The space that remains between the compost's surface and the pot's rim is essential if the plant is to be watered properly. If too small, insufficient water is applied (or more frequent watering is necessary) and if excessively deep too much water is applied and the compost becomes very wet.

Plants in 6–13cm/2$\frac{1}{2}$–5in-wide pots need a 12mm/$\frac{1}{2}$in watering space, while those in 14–19cm/ 5$\frac{1}{2}$–7$\frac{1}{2}$in pots need a space of 18mm/$\frac{3}{4}$in. As the sizes of pots increase, so do the spaces. Plants in 20–23cm/8–9in pots need 2.5cm/1in spaces and those in 25–30cm/10–12in ones need a gap of 36mm/1$\frac{1}{2}$in.

REPOTTING

Remove the plant from its existing pot by placing a hand over the soil ball, inverting the plant and knocking the rim on a hard surface. If a plant is exceptionally pot-bound (masses of roots around

1. REPOTTING *a plant when its roots become congested is essential to prevent growth ceasing. Remove the pot by placing a hand over the soil ball, inverting it and tapping the rim on a firm surface.*

2. SELECT *a clean, slightly larger pot. Place and firm a handful of compost in its base. Stand the plant on top and adjust the compost so that the top of the soil ball is about 12mm/1/2in below the rim.*

3. TRICKLE *and firm fresh potting compost around the soil ball. Ensure a gap is left at the top of the pot so that the compost can be watered. Lightly tap the pot's side to level loose compost on the surface.*

the sides of the root-ball) it may be necessary to run a knife between the side of the pot and the ball of roots.

If the plant is in a clay pot there might be a small piece of broken clay pot (known as a crock) in its base. This is placed over the drainage hole in the pot's base to prevent compost escaping. If the crock is present, remove it.

Exceptionally congested plants will have masses of matted roots; tease these out and remove old, dead ones.

Always choose a clean, dry pot in a suitable size. If a clay pot is being used, place a crock – concave-side downwards – over the drainage hole. Plastic pots do not require to be crocked. Fill and

REPOTTING CACTI

Many cacti have stiff, sharp spines and therefore need to be handled with respect and care. When repotting them, wrap a piece of folded newspaper around the stem to form a temporary handle.

firm compost in the base and stand the soil ball on it. Adjust its height so that the soil ball's top leaves a gap below the rim (see earlier for the right space).

Trickle compost around the soil ball and firm it gently but firmly with your fingers. Ensure that the plant is placed in the centre of the pot.

Water the compost carefully to prevent it being washed out of the pot. It may be necessary to fill the watering gap several times. Insert a plant label into the compost.

DOUBLE POTTING

To keep the roots of some tropical and sub tropical plants cool, some of them are double-potted. This involves using clay pots and placing one pot inside another, with the 12–18mm/$1/2$ – $3/4$ in space between them filled with damp peat. This space is then continually kept moist.

AFTER repotting, place plants in attractive outer containers known as cache *pots. Choose a colour and shape that enhances the plant, rather than dominating it. Here is* Aspidistra elatior, *widely known as Cast Iron Plant or Bar-room Plant.*

PLANTS FOR
COLD GREENHOUSES
❖

COLD greenhouses have no artificial heat in winter. However, with good insulation – especially on cold and windward sides – the temperature should not fall much below freezing.

The temperature in unheated conservatories does not usually fall as quickly or as low as free-standing greenhouses: warm house walls help to prevent rapid fluctuations in temperature.

Positioning plants in the centre of a greenhouse or conservatory helps to protect them during exceptionally cold weather. Cold draughts are especially damaging, and therefore ensure doors and ventilators fit their frames tightly.

CAMELLIAS *(above)*
are evergreen shrubs,
with beautiful flowers
in early spring.
Aspidistras (left) are
popular houseplants.

RANGE OF PLANTS
There are many ornamental plants that survive low temperatures, and while most are grown for their attractive foliage, others are famed for their flowers. Here are a few plants to consider:
• *Acorus gramineus:* the Grassy-leaved Sweet Flag grows 30–38cm/12–15in high in a pot,

with narrow, leathery, green leaves. The form 'Variegatus' is more attractive, with the narrow leaves being striped white.
• *Aspidistra elatior:* the Cast Iron Plant is famed for its tolerance of neglect, but when well grown is superb. There is a beautifully variegated form with cream stripes on its leaves.
• *Aucuba japonica* 'Variegata': the Spotted Laurel is an evergreen shrub that when small is ideal in cool conservatories and greenhouses. The shiny, green leaves have yellow spots.
• *Camellia japonica:* the Common Camellia is a delight in late winter and early spring, with large, waxy flowers. Avoid any sudden changes in the temperature or fluctuations of moisture in the compost.
• *Campanula isophylla:* the Star of Bethlehem is very floriferous, creating a wealth of star-like flowers during mid- and late summer. It is ideal for growing in a hanging basket as well as in a pot.

THE *Spotted Laurel*
(above) is ideal in
unheated rooms and
greenhouses. The
Grassy-leaved Sweet
Flag also thrives in
unheated places.

• *Chlorophytum comosum:* the Spider Plant is well-known for its narrow, white-and-green cascading leaves. Plant it in a pot where the stems can trail freely.

• *Crocus chrysanthus:* this diminutive crocus can be planted in bowls in late summer and early autumn. The bulbs must be allowed to grow naturally, with no artificial heat. They flower in late winter and early spring.

• Daffodils: These have large flowers and are distinguished from other narcissi by their trumpets which are as long as, or longer than, the petals. Bulbs are planted in late summer or early autumn for flowering from late winter to early spring.

• *Fatsia japonica:* the evergreen False Castor Oil Plant grows outdoors in sheltered areas and makes a good low-temperature plant for both greenhouses and conservatories.

• *Hedera helix:* there are many attractively variegated forms of this small-leaved ivy. They are ideal for growing up small canes or plastic trellis. They also trail.

Mother of Thousands (above) creates a remarkable display of trailing stems, while the False Castor Oil Plant (left) has large, hand-like leaves. It can also be grown outdoors in temperate climates.

• *Hedera canariensis* 'Variegata': also known as 'Gloire de Marengo' and the Canary Island Ivy. This ivy has large, dark green leaves merging through silvery-grey to white at the edges.

• *Hyacinthus orientalis:* hyacinths are famed for their stiff, upright, soldier-like appearance and sweetly-scented flowers, which appear from mid-winter to spring.

• *Iris danfordiae:* this dwarf, bulbous iris is well known for its honey-scented, lemon-yellow flowers that appear in mid- and late winter. Its flower stems are about 10cm/4in long, making it ideal for growing in pots and shallow pans in a cold greenhouse.

• *Iris reticulata:* another dwarf, bulbous iris, with deep bluish-purple flowers in late winter and early spring. The flower stems are about 15cm/6in long.

• *Saxifraga stolonifera:* widely known as the Mother of Thousands and Strawberry Geranium, this trailing plant never ceases to capture attention with its somewhat rounded leaves and thread-like trailing stems that bear young plants. The form 'Tricolor' has leaves variegated pink and pale yellow.

The Star of Bethlehem (left) develops blue, star-like flowers during mid- and late summer. There is also a white form.

The well-known Spider Plant (right) eventually needs a hanging basket or pedestal to enable stems to hang freely.

PLANTS FOR
COOL GREENHOUSES

❖

Cool greenhouses are where the temperature does not fall below 7°C/45°F in winter. This enables a much wider range of plants to be grown than in cold greenhouses. Some plants do not need warmth throughout winter, as they are raised from seeds sown in late winter or early spring.

THE *leaves of the Flame Nettle (left) appear beautifully painted in a vast array of vivid colours. It is raised from cuttings or seeds.*

RANGE OF PLANTS

There are many attractively flowered plants to choose from, as well as foliage types: some are permanent residents in greenhouses, while others live out their lives from spring to autumn, then die. Here are a few plants to consider:
• *Begonia semperflorens:* the Wax Begonia is ideal for decorating greenhouses, homes and gardens with flowers – white, through pink to red – from early to late summer. Sow seeds (no need to cover) in 16–20°C/61–68°F during late winter or early spring.
• *Begonia x tuberhybrida:* a tuberous-rooted begonia with large, rose-like flowers from early to late

THE *dome-like flowers heads of Cinerarias (right) are dominant and bright, from early winter to early summer.*

THE *bright, small, orchid-like flowers of the Butterfly Flower (left) swamp plants from spring to early summer.*

THE SILVERY INCH PLANT *(right) has green-and-silver bands along its glistening leaves. It is attractive throughout the year.*

summer. The tubers are packed into boxes of moist peat in early spring and started into growth. When shoots are about 5cm/2in high, move the plants into 13cm/5in wide pots.
• *Begonia x tuberhybrida* 'Pendula': this is the Basket Begonia, tuberous-rooted and with a trailing habit. It is ideal for growing in hanging-baskets.
• *Calceolaria x herbeohybrida:* the Slipper Flower, with masses of pouch-like flowers in bright colours from late spring to mid-summer and used to decorate homes as well as greenhouses and conservatories (see pages 36/37 for sowing seeds).
• *Senecio cruentus:* Cinerarias are superb plants for homes and greenhouses, developing dome-like heads of flowers from early winter to early summer (see pages 36/37 for sowing seeds).
• *Coleus blumei:* Flame Nettles are ideal foliage plants for a green-

house or home. Either take 7.5cm/3in long cuttings in late summer and insert in equal parts moist peat and sharp sand, or sow seeds in mid-winter in 16°C/61°F.

• _Cyclamen persicum:_ Cyclamen flower from late summer to mid-winter (see pages 36/37 for sowing seeds).

• _Primula obconica:_ the Poison Primula flowers from early winter to late spring (see pages 36/37 for sowing seeds).

• _Primula malacoides:_ the Fairy Primrose flowers from early winter to early spring (see pages 36/37 for sowing seeds).

• _Schizanthus pinnatus:_ the Butterfly Flower creates masses of flowers in greenhouses during spring and early summer. Sow seeds from mid- to late summer, 3mm/⅛in deep and in 16°C/61°F.

• _Sinningia speciosa:_ the well-known Gloxinia is superb in homes and conservatories, as well as greenhouses, and flowers from late spring to mid-summer. Sow seeds from mid-winter to early spring, just pressing them into the surface. When large enough to handle, prick out the seedlings into seed-

THE _Tuberous Begonia_ (above) creates a feast of large, rose-like flowers in many colours from early to late summer.

THE _Poison Primrose_ (above) develops masses of flowers in shades of pink, red, lilac from early winter to late spring.

trays, later moving them into pots.

• _Tradescantia fluminensis:_ the Wandering Jew is a well-known trailing plant, ideal in pots positioned at the edges of shelves so that stems can cascade.

• _Zebrina pendula:_ the Silvery Inch Plant has leaves up to 5cm/2in long, with glistening surfaces and green-and-silver bands.

As well as being grown in cool greenhouses and conservatories, the trailing _Tradescantia fluminensis_ and _Zebrina pendula_ can be planted in hanging-baskets and displayed in cool lobbies and porches during summer.

SLIPPER FLOWERS (right) have masses of pouch-like flowers in a rich range of colours from late spring to mid-summer.

CYCLAMEN (left) are popular flowering plants, with flowers at the tops of long stems from late summer to mid-winter.

SAVING MONEY

Use a heated propagator in winter to provide the temperature needed to germinate seedlings. This saves heating the entire greenhouse to a high temperature. Electric and paraffin heated types are available.

PLANTS FOR WARM GREENHOUSES
❖

WARM greenhouses and conservatories are expensive to heat during winter, but the wide range of tropical and subtropical plants that can be grown is wide and includes many plants that are sure to please you. Night temperatures of about 16°C/61°F are needed, with those during the day a few degrees higher. Additionally, the atmosphere needs to be humid. Plants to consider include:

• _Acalypha hispida:_ the Red-hot Cat's-tail eventually has a shrub-like stance, but when young can be grown in a pot. During summer, long tassels packed with red flowers hang from stems. A minimum night temperature about 16°C/61°F is essential, 18–24°C/64–75° during the day. Mist spray the leaves frequently to create a humid atmosphere.

• _Anthurium andreanum:_ the Painter's Palette is very distinctive, with shiny-green, heart-shaped leaves and flowers that resemble a painter's palette. These are red,

CROTONS _(below) are well known plants with leaves that display a wealth of colours. It is also known as Joseph's Coat._

THE PEACOCK PLANT _(above) has gloriously coloured, paper-thin leaves. Earlier, it was known as_ Maranta makoyana.

THE FROSTED SONERILA _(above) reveals coppery green leaves with silvery spots, while mature_ Black Gold Philodendrons _have large, dark green leaves with a coppery sheen and ivory veins._

with a straight, central spire about 5cm/2in long. Do not let the temperature fall below 16°C/61°F in winter. Mist spray plants regularly.

• _Anthurium crystallinum:_ the Crystal Anthurium has gloriously-coloured, large, velvety, dark green leaves with veins lined in ivory. Keep the night temperature in winter at 16°C/61°F or above.

• _Caladium x hortulanum_: the Angel's Wings has arrow-shaped, paper-thin leaves up to 30cm/12in long, in many bright colours. There are several named varieties. High temperatures are essential, never below 16°C/61°F and preferably about 21°C/70°F. Plants die down in late summer and the tubers are replanted in early spring. At this time, moist compost and a temperature about 24°C/75°F is needed. Mist spray plants regularly.

• _Calathea makoyana:_ the Peacock Plant is one of the prettiest of all foliage plants, with paper-thin leaves beautifully patterned silvery green and edged in mid-green. From below there are zones of purple or red. Temperatures of at least 16°C/61°F are needed, and avoid rapid fluctuations.

• *Calathea zebrina:* the Zebra Plant has narrowly oblong, soft emerald-green leaves banded in dark green. These bands appear as purple on the undersides. It is slightly easier to grow than the Peacock Plant, but nevertheless needs a minimum temperature of about 16°C/61°F.

• *Codiaeum variegatum:* the well-known Croton is also called Joseph's Coat, which very much describes the richness and varied nature of the thick leaves. The shapes of the leaves vary widely and there are many named varieties. A minimum temperature not less than 16°C/61°F is needed in winter, together with regular mist spraying.

• *Philodendron melanochrysum:* the Black Gold Philodendron was earlier known as *P. andreanum*. It has

RED-HOT CAT'S-TAIL *(below) develops long, tassel-like stems packed with bright red flowers. Its other name is Chenille Plant.*

THE *Painter's Palette (above) has large, heart-like leaves and shiny red, waxy 'palettes' with straight, central tails. A close relative, the Flamingo Flower, has curly tails.*

large, dark green leaves with a coppery sheen and veins lined in ivory. Mature leaves are up to 60cm/2ft long. When young, however, the plant has juvenile leaves, heart-shaped and velvety dark green. It needs a minimum winter temperature in the region of 18°C/64°F.

• *Sonerila margaritacea:* the Frosted Sonerila has coppery green leaves with silvery spots. A minimum winter temperature of 18°C/64°F is needed to enable plants to survive in good condition.

• *Syngonium podophyllum:* the Goose Foot Plant, also known as Arrowhead Vine and Nephthytis, has a climbing nature and needs a minimum winter temperature of 16°C/61°F. It has juvenile and adult leaves. When young, they are arrow shaped, but with age develop ears and lobes. There are several named forms, some attractively variegated. Occasionally, these plants are sold under the name *Nephthytis podophyllum*.

COPPER LEAF *(below right) creates a wealth of leaves mottled in many bright colours. Angel's Wings (below) has large, arrow-shaped, paper-thin leaves in many colours − and borne on long stems.*

GROWING MELONS
AND TOMATOES

❖

 MELONS are easily grown in greenhouses in summer, but to encourage early crops warmth is essential.

- Raising new plants: Sow seeds 12mm/1/2in deep, singly and on their sides, in small pots containing seed compost in mid- to late spring. Water and place in a propagator at 18°C/64°F. Cover with newspaper. Alternatively, cover several pots with a piece of glass, then newspaper. As soon as seeds germinate, remove the newspaper and place the pots in a warm, lightly shaded position. Keep the compost lightly moist but not waterlogged. When a plant has four leaves, pinch out the growing tip to just above the highest one.
- Planting: Put young melon plants in a greenhouse as soon as it is free from frost. Alternatively, use a heater until the weather improves, keeping the night temperature at least 13°C/55°F.

Plant them 45cm/11/2ft apart on mounds or ridges in the greenhouse soil. Alternatively, put two plants in a large growing-bag.

- Supporting: Secure horizontal wires, 30cm/12in apart, from 15cm/6in above the soil to about 1.8m/6ft high. Insert two long bamboo canes,15cm/6in on either side of each plant, and secure to the top wire. These provide the main supports. However, before the plants reach the first wire, support them with short canes tied to the lowest wire. When plants reach the first wire, pinch out their growing tips and train a sideshoot on both sides to grow along the wire and up the canes.
- Stopping: when shoots reach the tops of canes, pinch out their tips to encourage sideshoots. These will then bear fruits. Pinch off the tips of side-shoots, one leaf beyond the female flower.
- Pollination and harvesting: see above right steps 4, 5 and 6.

1. SOW *melon seeds singly in 6.5–7.5cm/2*1/2*–3in-wide pots, filled and firmed with moist potting compost. Insert each seed on its side and about 12mm/*1/2*in deep; water and place the pots in 18°C/64°F.*

2. PLACE *in a propagator or cover with glass and newspaper. Remove these after germination and lower the temperature. When four leaves have developed, pinch out the growing tip above the fourth leaf.*

3. IN *late spring, plant them 45cm/1*1/2*ft apart on slight mounds or ridges in a greenhouse border. Support the young stems with bamboo canes secured to a horizontal wire. Maintain 13°C/55°F at night.*

4. AS *plants grow, train main stems on canes. These later produce sideshoots. Female flowers have small, round, bulges behind them: males are straight. Dust pollen from male flowers into the female ones.*

5. SWELLING *melons need support. Secure a net under each one, giving it firm support while ripening. If melons on low shoots are lying on the ground, place them on large, clean upturned flower pots.*

6. HARVEST *melons when the end opposite the stalk is softening. By then, the characteristic melon scent with be obvious. Cut each fruit carefully, severing it from the stalk, and eat without too much delay.*

GROWING TOMATOES

Tomato plants cannot be planted into an unheated greenhouse until all risk of frost has passed.

• <u>Raising plants</u>: Sow seeds 12mm/1/2in deep in seed-trays during mid- to late spring and place in 16–18°C/61–64°F. Water and put the pots in a propagator. Cover them with newspaper. Germination takes seven to ten days. Then remove the paper and slightly lower the temperature. When large enough to handle, prick out the seedlings into individual pots.

• <u>Planting and feeding</u>: Set plants in growing-bags or large pots. Support the plants with canes and wires and feed them every ten days from when the first truss (bunch fruit) is formed.

• <u>Sideshooting and stopping</u>: Remove all shoots growing in the angles of the leaves – snap them sideways. In late summer, pinch out the growing tip. Also, gradually remove lower leaves to help ripen the fruits.

• <u>Harvesting</u>: Pick when ripe.

TOMATOES *are ideal in greenhouses and return the attention they need with many pounds of fruits throughout summer and into autumn.*

ORCHIDS

❖

There are two basic types of orchid: those that live at ground level in soil and are known as *terrestrial*, and those that grow on trees and shrubs and are known as *epiphytic*. Terrestrial species are mainly native to temperate regions, while epiphytic ones are tropical or subtropical. Most orchids grown in greenhouses and conservatories are epiphytic.

GROWING
EPIPHYTIC ORCHIDS

Although they have a delicate appearance, orchids are remarkably hardy. Some can be encouraged to flower indoors, but a greenhouse or conservatory is needed for their resting period.

• Resting period: Most epiphytic orchids grow during summer and rest in winter, growth ceasing and the plant relying on food reserves stored in pseudobulbs (thick stem bases, but not true bulbs). During this period, place the plant in full light and keep the compost relatively dry until new growth begins. A clue to the onset of an orchid's resting period is the shedding of some leaves, but this varies according to the species.

• Compost: Proprietary compost mixtures for epiphytic orchids are available. Alternatively, use a potting mixture formed of finely-ground bark, moist peat, sphagnum moss and vermiculite.

• Potting: Keep epiphytic orchids in small pots and repot them after flowering has finished or when new growth and roots appear. Repotting is illustrated below. Allow a week to pass before watering a newly-potted plant.

1. REPOTTING *orchids is an important part of growing them. To remove the soil ball from the pot, place a hand over it, invert the pot and tap its rim very sharply on a firm surface.*

2. GENTLY *tease away old compost from between the roots. At the same time, cut away dead roots, as well as overlong ones that might be damaged when the plant is repotted.*

3. SELECT *a clean pot, the same size or fractionally larger than before. Place drainage material in its base, hold the plant in place, fill and firm the compost around it.*

SHADING *is essential. Slatted wooden blinds are the best as they can be rolled down during hot weather and raised when dull. Light is essential to ripen resting orchid plants.*

TO CREATE *a humid atmosphere, especially during exceptionally hot days, gently mist spray between the staging. This also cools the roots of plants and reduces watering frequency.*

WHEN *orchids are displayed near open ventilators they will dry out very rapidly. Orchids near heating pipes also dry quickly. Check the compost frequently to ensure it is not dry.*

- <u>Watering:</u> During its period of active growth, the compost in which epiphytic orchids are growing must be kept moist. Plunge the entire root area in a bucket of clean water every three or four days during summer. During cool periods, only once a week is necessary.
- <u>Feeding:</u> Orchids are fed during late spring and summer, but they vary in their needs – consult a specialist nursery when buying them. Take care, as excessive food kills them.
- <u>Humidity:</u> In summer, mist spraying is essential to create a humid atmosphere. Lightly syringe the foliage, as well as between the pots and on the floor, three or four times a day.
- <u>Shade:</u> Orchids need shade during periods of strong sunlight, from early spring to late summer. Slatted wooden blinds are best, as they can be rolled up and down to suit the weather. Light, however, is needed to ripen resting orchid plants.
- <u>Temperatures:</u> The temperature requirements for orchids varies from one species to another, although they can be classified into three broad groups.

1. Cool – not less than 10°C/50°F at night and rising to a maximum temperature 24°C/75°F during the day in summer.

2. Intermediate – not less than 13°C/55°F at night and rising to a maximum 24°C/75°F during the day in summer.

3. Warm – not less that 18°C/64°F at night and preferably 21°C/70°F. Also, a rise of several degrees during the day.

DISPLAYING ORCHIDS

Apart from growing orchids in pots and placing them on slatted staging in a greenhouse, display them by securing them to pieces of attractive wood or thick bark. Place a pad of sphagnum moss or osmunda fibre between the orchid and wood, and secure them together with plastic-covered wire. Another attractive way is to form a hanging basket from wooden slats and to plant an orchid in it. Ready-made baskets can be bought from specialist suppliers.

CLOCHES AND
GARDEN FRAMES

❖

CLOCHES are versatile, enabling crops to be protected during their early stages as well as later when maturing. As well, they are used in late winter and early spring to warm up strips of land in preparation for sowing seeds.

The range of cloches has increased dramatically in recent years. In addition to glass, rigid plastic types are widely available, as well as those covered with polythene sheeting.

• Tent cloches are formed of two pieces of glass held together at their tops with wires that also form handles. In most tent cloches glass is used, but plastic is also available. Also, rigid netting is sometimes secured under the plastic, which when removed leaves plants protected from birds.

Because tent cloches are relatively low they are only suitable for warming soil, initial sowing and raising plants, and for low, salad- type crops. Ensure the ends of the row are blocked to prevent it becoming a wind-tunnel.

• Barn cloches are higher than tent types and formed of four sheets of glass held together with wires that also form handles. Crops are ventilated by opening one of the roof panes. These cloches function in the same way as tent types, but with the benefit of covering taller crops. Blocking off the ends of the row is important, as they are less stable than tent types.

• Corrugated PVC plastic cloches are strong and light, but they must be well secured to the ground to prevent them blowing away. Their uses are the same as tent types. Ventilation is created by removing every other cloche during the day. Storing them is not a problem as they are soon dismantled and stored flat.

• Polythene tunnels create inexpensive protection for seeds while germinating, young plants and low salad crops. They are bought as kits and easily assembled by stretching a sheet of polythene over wire hoops anchored in the

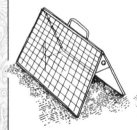

TENT CLOCHES *are made of two panes of glass secured with wires. New types have netting secured under a plastic cover: with the covering removed the netting gives protection in summer against birds.*

BARN CLOCHES *are formed from four sheets of glass, supported by a thick wire frame. One side of the roof can be opened to increase the amount of ventilation. There is a wire handle at each cloche's top.*

CORRUGATED PVC *combines strength with lightness. Because of their light weight they are folded around half-moon metal frames with spikes on their lower ends. These are pushed into the soil.*

POLYTHENE TUNNELS *are inexpensive and increasingly popular, although the polythene has to be replaced fairly frequently. It is secured over metal hoops, then held down by thin wires.*

OLD, PLASTIC UMBRELLAS, *as well as clear bottles with their bases cut out, make cheap covers for plants during spring. They do, however, need to be well secured by pegs or wire hooks into the soil.*

DUTCH LIGHTS, *mounted on a wooden base, create ideal places in which to acclimatize summer-bedding plants to outdoor life. Lettuces and other low-growing salad crops can be grown in them.*

ground. Thin wires are put over the top to secure the polythene.

It is an excellent way to provide protection on rows 6m/20ft or more long. The life of polythene is variable, but usually not more than two years: it deteriorates in sunlight and is soon ripped. If in good condition at the end of the year, wash and allow to dry before storing. Ventilation is provided by rolling up the side away from the prevailing wind.

• Recycled clear plastic umbrellas make excellent temporary protections for plants, but they must be anchored securely into the soil. Plastic bottles and containers – with their bases cut out – are other possibilities and worth using in an effort to conserve natural resources.

• Dutch lights, about 1.5m/5ft long and 75cm/2½ft wide, are ideal for forming garden frames in which plants can be acclimatized to outdoor conditions after being raised in greenhouses. Salad crops, such as lettuces, can also be grown in them. Each frame is

formed of a single sheet of glass secured in a wooden frame. These are placed on a south-facing, sloping, wood or brick base: 20cm/8in at the front and 30cm/12in at the back.

BELL-SHAPED CLOCHES

Bell-shaped glass cloches with a knob on the top for handling were used in the early seventeenth century. The term 'cloche' is derived from the French and means a bell or dish-cover.

Earthenware jars have also been used to cover plants, especially in winter and to encourage blanching.

PESTS AND DISEASES

❖

WHENEVER plants grow in confined groups – and especially if there is a large number of a similar type together – pests and diseases soon arrive. Some can be prevented by propagating only from healthy plants or by keeping the greenhouse clean and free from rubbish. Other precautions include using clean compost, ensuring good ventilation but not draughts, maintaining correct temperatures, buying only healthy plants and ensuring the compost does not become excessively wet or too dry. Also, do not leave dead flowers on plants as they encourage pests and diseases.

It is an accurate observation that insects have only two ambitions – sex and eating. It is therefore essential to be vigilant and to control them as quickly as possible, before epidemic proportions are reached.

GREENFLY *(aphids) pierce the soft parts of plants, sucking sap and causing mottling and distortion. Spray regularly with malathion, dimethoate or resmethrin and pyrethrum.*

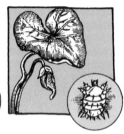

CYCLAMEN MITES *are dust-like spiders that infest plants. Leaves curl and wrinkle, plants are stunted. Remove and burn seriously infected plants. Spray with malathion or insectidal soap.*

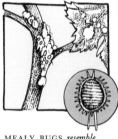

MEALY BUGS *resemble white, waxy woodlice. They suck sap, causing distortion and yellowing. Wipe off small colonies with cotton swabs dipped in methylated spirits (rubbing alcohol).*

SCALE INSECTS *create waxy-brown discs under which young ones are produced. They suck sap, causing speckling. Destroy badly infected plants or treat as for mealy bugs.*

EARWIGS *feed at night, chewing and tearing flowers and soft leaves. Pick off and destroy all earwigs; trap in inverted pots filled with straw and on top of canes or spray with malathion.*

RED SPIDER MITES *suck sap, causing mottling and, eventually, webs. Leaves drop prematurely. Syringe plants regularly and spray with derris or insecticidal soap.*

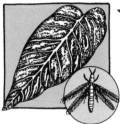

THRIPS *are tiny flies that jump or fly from leaf to leaf, causing silvery streaks on leaves. Flowers become distorted. Spray with malathion or derris. Worse when compost is dry.*

WHITEFLIES *are small and moth-like. They suck sap, causing yellowing and leaves to fall off. When disturbed they flutter about. Spray regularly with malathion or pyrethrum.*

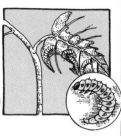

CATERPILLARS *of many types infest greenhouses, chewing soft leaves and stems. Look under leaves. Pick off and destroy them. Also, remove severely infected plants. Spray with derris.*

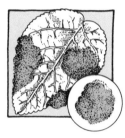

BOTRYTIS *(grey mould) is a fungal disease entering plants through cuts and wounds. Encouraged by damp, still air and excessive watering. Remove dead flowers. Use a fungicide.*

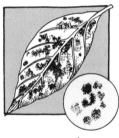

SOOTY MOULD *is a fungus that grows on honeydew excreted by aphids and other sap-sucking insects. Wipe off light infestation on smooth leaves. Control sap-sucking pests.*

BLACK LEG *is a disease of cuttings, especially pelargoniums. Stem bases become soft and black. Encouraged by cold, wet, compacted and airless compost. Destroy.*

POWDERY MILDEW *coats leaves with a white, dust-like coating – often on both sides. Remove badly infected parts, increase ventilation and keep the atmosphere drier.*

RUST *is not very common but occasionally seen on greenhouse plants, creating raised rings of brown or black spores. Remove and burn infected leaves and increase ventilation.*

VIRUSES *infect many plants and although they seldom kill, their host's vigour is reduced. Aphids and other sap-sucking pests spread them. Therefore, eradicate all pests.*

GREENHOUSE CALENDAR

❖

Numbers in brackets are page references

SPRING

This is an active time in the greenhouses.

- Check that automatic ventilators open freely (22-23)
- Ensure compost, pots, seed-trays and other pieces of equipment are available for sowing seeds and taking cuttings (24-25)
- Wherever possible, install automatic watering devices to ensure plants are always adequately watered (26-27)
- Mist-propagation units make rooting cuttings easy and quick. Install amateur units now (27)
- Take soft-wood cuttings in spring (34-35)
- Take leaf-stem cuttings (34)
- Sow cacti seeds (37)
- Sow Cineraria (*Senecio cruentus*) seeds (36-37)
- Sow Flaming Katy (*Kalanchoë blossfeldiana*) seeds (37)
- Sow Slipper Flower (*Calceolaria x herbeohybrida*) in late spring (37)
- Sow Poison Primrose (*Primula obconica*) in early spring (37)
- Sow Fairy Primrose (*Primula malacoides*) in early spring (37)
- Sow Chinese Primrose (*Primula sinensis*) seeds in early spring (37)
- Sow Wax Begonia (*Begonia semperflorens*) seeds during late winter and early spring (46-47)
- Start *Begonia x tuberhybrida* into growth (46-47)
- In early spring, check that the staging is firm. At this time of year – and during summer – slatted staging is better then solid types (16)
- As the weather improves in late spring, regularly damp down the floor and staging (23)
- Take cuttings of chrysanthemums (34-35)
- During late spring and summer, feed epiphytic orchids (54-55)

SUMMER

Providing the correct temperatures for plants is important: if too high, plants are soon damaged.

- Install shading – either painting proprietary shading liquid over the outside or fitting roller blinds (22-23)
- In conservatories, Venetian-type blinds can be fitted to the inside to decrease the sun's glare and to reduce temperatures (22-23)
- Sow Cyclamen (*Cyclamen persicum*) seeds (36)
- Sow Cineraria (*Senecio cruentus*) seeds (36-37)
- Sow Slipper Flowers (*Calceolaria x herbeohybrida*) in early and mid-summer (37)
- Prick out seedlings when large enough to handle (40-41)
- Pot up the young plants when they fill their container with roots (42-43)
- Shade epiphytic orchids in summer (54-55)
- Repot plants when they fill existing pots with roots (44-45)
- During late spring and summer, most epiphytic orchids need feeding (54-55)
- Take cuttings of Flame Nettles (*Coleus blumei*) (46-47)
- Dampen orchid houses in summer, both on the floor and between the pots (54-55)
- Sow Butterfly Flower (*Schizanthus pinnatus*) seeds in mid- to late summer (46-47)
- In early summer, pack away heaters and store in a dry shed.
- Regularly dampen down the floor and between pots to create a moist atmosphere. Take care not to moisten flowers or soft, hairy leaves (23).
- Most epiphytic orchids grow in summer and therefore need regular watering (54-55)

AUTUMN

By autumn, many plants have finished flowering or have been harvested. It is therefore a time of clearing up and ensuring plants ridden with pests or diseases are not left to spread these problems in the following year. Therefore, burn infected plants.

If the border soil is contaminated, this will need replacing with fresh garden soil or potting compost. This can be prohibitively expensive and therefore it is much easier to grow plants in growing-bags or pots placed on the border soil in a greenhouse.

Take down, pack away and store shading blinds from the outsides of greenhouses. Plastic types will need to be washed to remove grime. Check that all strings and pulleys are in good order.

Where the cost of heating during the previous winter was costly, consider planting a hedge. A deciduous one formed of bare-rooted plants can be planted at any time from late autumn to early spring. If, however, you decide an evergreen hedge is better, plant this in late spring if in a 'balled' form. Plants growing in containers can be planted at any time when the soil is not frozen or waterlogged.

- Insulate the insides of greenhouses (20-21)
- Check ventilators and doors to ensure they fit properly and do not allow draughts to enter and blow on plants (20-21)
- If planning the construction of a greenhouse, ensure its orientation is correct (20-21)
- Clean the glass, removing whitening materials used to create shade during summer (22-23). This may need several stiff brushings and plenty of water. The sun will have baked it on the glass.

WINTER

In some areas, winter is no more than a few frosts, while in others it is snowdrifts and ice-covered paths. If snow covers your greenhouse roof and it is not too deep, leave it there. However, if it remains for too long, use a soft, long-handled broom to remove it. Leaving it in position acts as an insulation from severe frosts, but it does prevent the entry of light.

- Where greenhouses are used throughout the year, the conservation of heat during winter is essential (20-21)
- If the greenhouse is empty, open all doors and ventilators to allow cold air to kill pests
- Have electrical equipment checked by a competent electrician to ensure it is safe and functioning properly
- Clean and disinfect pots and seed-trays ready for use in spring. Store them in a clean shed, away from rubbish
- Use a plastic label or thin piece of metal to scrape dirt out of the overlaps in the glass. Wash with soapy water, then hose down the outside
- Sow Wax Begonia (*Begonia semperflorens*) seeds during late winter and early spring (46-47)
- Sow seeds of the colourfully-leafed Flame Nettle (*Coleus blumei*) in mid-winter (46-47)
- In late winter, fit temporary shelves into roofs of greenhouses so that extra seed-trays and pots can be accommodated at seed sowing time (17)
- In winter, solid staging is better than slatted types (16)
- Winter is the time when most epiphytic orchids are resting (54-55). Keep their compost relatively dry during this dormant period..
- Check the temperature given to epiphytic orchids (54-55)

USEFUL
GREENHOUSE TERMS
❖

AUTOMATIC VENTILATOR: *A ventilator that automatically opens and closes in reaction to a change in temperature.*

BARN CLOCHE: *A tall cloche, formed of four sheets of glass with a wire frame.*

BOTTOM HEAT: *Warming a rooting mixture from below.*

BUBBLE GLAZING: *A method of insulating a greenhouse with plastic.*

CAPILLARY WATERING: *A method of watering plants: water in a moisture-retentive base passes into compost in pots.*

CLOCHE: *Originally, a bell-shaped cover used to protect plants. Now, it means a wide range of low glass or plastic-covered structures.*

COLD FRAME: *A low framework covered with a Dutch light or similar structure.*

CONSERVATORY: *Originally used to indicate a glass structure where plants were 'conserved'. Now, usually means a lean-to glass structure where growing plants is combined with a leisure area.*

COMPOST: *Refers to the mixture in which cuttings are inserted, seeds sown and plants replanted. Can also refer to decomposed vegetative material.*

CUTTING: *A method of vegetative propagation, by which a severed part is encouraged to form roots.*

DAMPING DOWN: *Spraying water on the floor or benches in a greenhouse to create a humid atmosphere.*

DIBBER: *Pencil-like, blunt-ended stick used to insert cuttings or transplant young seedlings.*

DUTCH LIGHT: *A large, single sheet of glass – about 1.5m/5ft x 75cm/2^1/2ft – secured in a wooden frame-work and placed on a low structure. Used to harden off plants as well as to grow low-growing salad vegetables.*

EVEN-SPAN GREENHOUSE: *Another name for full-span.*

EXTRACTOR FAN: *Used to draw hot air out of a greenhouse, sunroom or modern conservatory.*

ENVIRONMENTALLY-FRIENDLY COMPOST: *Formed of materials other than peat or loam (good quality soil). Some new composts are created from the outer husks of coconuts.*

FAN HEATER: *An electrically-powered fan, used to warm a greenhouse.*

FLAT: *North American term for seed-tray.*

FRAME: *Usually refers to a cold frame.*

FULL-SPAN: *A greenhouse with equal amounts of glass on both sides of the central ridge bar.*

GLASSHOUSE: *Commercial horticultural term for a large type of greenhouse.*

GLAZING BARS: *Structural bars in the roof and sides of a greenhouse which support the glass.*

GREENHOUSE: *Originally, a glass-covered structure where plants were kept 'green' during winter. Now, a place where plants can be grown throughout the year, using heating.*

GROWING-BAG: *A large, plastic bag filled with a peat and fertilizer mixture in which plants can be grown quickly and easily, without soil preparation.*

HARDENING OFF: *Acclimatizing plants to outdoor conditions.*

KEROSENE HEATERS: *North American term for paraffin heaters.*

LEAN-TO: *A greenhouse constructed against a wall, preferably a warm one.*

LOAM-BASED COMPOSTS: *Formed of loam (good quality soil), peat and sand, plus fertilizers.*

LONG-SPOUTED WATERING-CANS: *Watering-cans with long necks that enable plants at the backs of benches to be watered.*

MINIMUM- AND MAXIMUM- THERMOMETER: *A thermometer that indicates the highest and lowest temperature since it was last read and reset.*

MINI-GREENHOUSE: *Small greenhouses, usually lean-to and with a depth of no more than 60cm/2ft.*

MIST-PROPAGATION: *A method of regularly covering cuttings with a fine mist spray of water to keep them cool, reduce transpiration and encourage rapid rooting.*

MIST SPRAYERS: *Used to create a humid atmosphere around plants.*

MOBILE GREEN-HOUSE: *A moveable, commercial glasshouse constructed on wheels.*

MOISTURE-INDICATOR STRIPS: *Inserted permanently in compost in a pot to indicate if a plant needs further water.*

MOISTURE-METERS: *A probe inserted into compost which indicates if a plant needs further water.*

ORANGERY: *Early glass-covered structure built to cover orange trees, especially in winter.*

OVER THE RIM WATERING: *Watering a plant by filling the gap between the compost and pot's rim with water.*

PARAFFIN (KEROSENE) HEATERS: *Heaters fuelled by paraffin – a popular way to heat a greenhouse.*

PEAT-BASED COMPOSTS: *Formed of granulated peat and various fertilizers.*

PEAT POTS: *Formed of fertilizers and compressed, rigid peat.*

PIT LIGHT: *An early type of horticultural frame.*

PLASTIC TUNNEL: *Large, metal hoops covered with clear or opaque flexible plastic sheeting.*

POT-BOUND: *Congested roots, an indication that repotting is needed.*

POTS: *Formed of either clay or plastic, and available in a wide range of sizes.*

POTTING ON: *Transferring a plant from one pot to another.*

POTTING UP: *Initially potting up a plant.*

PRICKING OUT: *The initial moving of seedlings from where they were sown into pots or seed-trays.*

PROPAGATION: *Increasing plants.*

PROPAGATORS: *Enclosed, plastic or glass-covered units in which seeds are encouraged to germinate and cuttings to root. Some are heated by electricity, others by paraffin (kerosene).*

REPOTTING: *Transferring a plant from its current pot to a larger one.*

ROLLER BLINDS: *A method of shading a green-house, sunroom or conservatory.*

SEED-TRAY: *Known in North America as a flat. Flat-based tray in which seeds are sown and seedlings pricked off.*

SHADING: *Reducing the amount of light entering a greenhouse to prevent the temperature rising and to stop plants being burned by strong sunlight.*

SHELVING: *Wooden or metal structures on which pots or seed-trays are placed.*

SPRIG: *A small, headless nail used to secure glass to a wooden-framed greenhouse.*

STAGING: *Either a solid or slatted framework at about waist height for supporting plants and working on.*

STOVE HOUSE: *An old term for a greenhouse that is kept at a high temperature.*

TENT CLOCHE: *A low cloche, formed of two sheets of glass. Some are made from plastic.*

TRICKLE IRRIGATION: *A method of constantly watering plants in greenhouses.*

SUNROOM: *A North American term for a conservatory.*

THERMOSTAT: *A device for controlling the operation of an electrically-powered heater or fan.*

THREE-QUARTER SPAN: *A greenhouse where the glass area on one side of the ridge bar is greater than on the other.*

TUBULAR HEATER: *An electrically-powered heater, in the form of a tube.*

VENTILATORS: *Hinged windows in the roofs and sides of greenhouses, conservatories and sunrooms.*

WARDIAN CASE: *A totally enclosed, mainly glass container. Originated by Dr. Nathaniel Ward.*

WINDOW CONSERVATORY: *Victorian construction, filling a window area with a small glasshouse.*

INDEX

❖